To: David,

You can

do it!

From:

This book is dedicated to:

My father who taught me and others, "You are more than you think you are,"

My mother who loved me when no one else did,

My wife who has allowed me to follow my dreams,

Rich Wilkins who has always seen more in me than I could,

Father Cyprian Davis who has been grace to my spirit, and to

the Anonymous Americans who by following their God given dreams have made me who and what I am today.

FOLLOW YOUR DREAMS

By

Conway

**Eight Steps for
Turning Your Dreams into Reality**

Follow Your Dreams:
Eight Steps for Turning Your Dreams into Reality

Copyright © 1995 by Conway Stone

All Rights Reserved

Published by D. Conway Stone,
500 Briar Hill Road, Louisville, KY 40206
Phone:1-888-899-5353
Quantity discounts available

With help from Passages Publishing,
P.O. Box 5093, Louisville, KY 40255

ISBN 1-886036-08-X

Library of Congress Number: 95-94784

Printed in the United States of America

TABLE OF CONTENTS

"What you want to do, and what you can do, is limited only by what you can dream."

Mike Melville

Forward

As I sit here putting the final touches on this manuscript, the University of Arkansas (one of my favorite basketball teams) is ripping it's way through March madness on it's way to the national championship game; it has been one of those perfect weeks where the sun is brightly shining and it's 70 degrees outside, and here I am stuck in an 8x8 room staring at a computer doing boring editorial work. I am reminded that there is a price to be paid to follow any dream.

It is my prayer that this book will inspire you to pay the price and follow your dreams.

Conway

SECTION I

Dreamers: Our only hope!

"The future belongs to those who believe in the beauty of their dreams."

Eleanor Roosevelt

Chapter 1
Anonymous Americans

Five....
  Four.....
    Three....
      Two.....
        One.....
          Blast Off!

Those were the words spoken July 14, 1969, when the United States of America shot 3,000 tons of fuel, metal and wires along with 3 astronauts into space heading for the moon. Perhaps the crowning proof of man's ability to turn its dreams into reality came two days later when on July 16th we landed two famous Americans on the moon.

Do you remember the name of the first man to put foot on the moon?_____?   Yes, his name was Neil Armstrong. Do you remember the name of the second man to put foot on the moon?_____? Yes, that's right his name was Buzz Aldrin.

If you have a good memory, you might be able to come up with the name of the third astronaut. Remember, he did not land on the moon; he stayed in the spacecraft and circled the moon while Armstrong and Aldrin went to the surface. Do you remember his name? _____? His name was Michael Collins.

Now for the hard part. Do you remember the name of the president of NASA in 1969? O.K. let's try another one. There was a lady who was in charge of all the computer programming for NASA in 1969. She figured out all the calculations it would take to send a man to the moon and bring him back safely. Do you know her name?_____? Well, there was a man in charge of running all the wires for NASA in 1969. He ran the wires that would start the engines of the space rocket when the right button was pushed. Do you recall his name? _____? O.K. one more. I'm sure you will know this one. There was a fellow in charge of haul-ing all the fuel for NASA in 1969. He went down to the local Texaco station (just kidding) and loaded up some fuel and hauled it to the launch pad. Do you recall his name? _____? No? Why not?

Well, with every endeavor there are always one or two famous people who get the credit and the glory for what happens. But behind the famous faces having their pictures taken with the President and behind every superstar earning the big salaries there are hundreds, if not thousands, of people who have made that pro-ject a success. We may not be able to recall their names, but our projects and dreams could not be successful without these Anonymous Americans.

What is an Anonymous American?

Anonymous Americans are people like you and me. People who are not rich and famous and who have not left the world any scientific achievements, but this world could not function without them. We, the Anonymous Americans of this country, make this country what it is.

Let's go back to our NASA illustration. Could NASA have put two famous Americans on the moon without the toil and sweat of the fellow who hauled the fuel for them or of the lady who did all the computer calculations? No! It took the work and effort of thousands of Anonymous Americans to put those two famous Americans on the moon.

In fact, would you like to guess how many Anonymous Americans NASA employed in 1969? What do you think...1,000? 2,000? 5,000? 10,000? Come on, they only put two men on the moon! In 1969 NASA employed 33,929 people. It took over 33,000 Anonymous Americans to put two famous Americans on the moon. We are the ones who make things happen!

If you want to calculate all the contractors and sub-contractors to the contractors, it took over 150,000 Anonymous Americans to make that moon landing possible. And I always have one person who comes up and reminds me that it took 100,000,000 taxpayers to put those two men on the moon.

The same story could be told for your work, church and school. There may be one or two famous people, like the president or the CEO, running around getting all the credit. There may be a couple of high-flying sales people earning much of the money in the company, but that company could not function without the secretaries, marketing people and average sales person. The company would fold without the work of Anonymous Americans.

In fact if our society is to overcome the enormous problems we face, we must get the rank and file, the Anonymous Americans, people like you and me involved in the process. The problem is that many of our Anonymous Americans are not involved in the process. Many Anonymous Americans are just wandering through life not taking full advantage of their abilities and power. They are as Henry David Thoreau said, "living lives of quiet desperation." I am convinced that the only hope we have to overcome the problems facing our families and society is for Anonymous Americans, people like you and me, to make a difference in this world by following our God given dreams.

So Anonymous Americans stand tall with me. Take pride in what you do and who you are. You make this world what it is. You are the ones who get the work done, make companies function and make dreams come true!

"If you can change your mind, you can change your life."

William James

Chapter 2

The story of one Anonymous American

I am an Anonymous American with deep roots in the American dream. I grew up in Arkansas in a great Christian home, playing softball on church teams, going to school and traveling to see my grandparents on holidays.

My father and I enjoyed a very unique relationship, because a college professor once told my father there would come a day when he and I would not be able to communicate. The college professor was talking about the teenage years, of course. My father vowed that this would never happen to him; he worked very hard to develop a healthy "confidant-type" relationship with me.

As a junior in high school, I discovered a passion for philosophy and psychology. In high school, I took every psychology and sociology class I could and delighted in the long discussions of religion and philosophy with my father around the dinner table and on long car rides. I took off for an Arkansas college in the fall of 1978 to study psychology.

My goals for going to college were simple. First, I wanted to get a degree in psychology so I could become a Christian psychologist. Second, I wanted to travel to a foreign country so I could see how people lived outside of my world. Third, I wanted to find a good southern girl I could marry and spend the rest of my life with. Yes, I was a dreamer even back then.

While in college, I worked summers at a YMCA conference center in Asheville, N.C. In my junior year I was elected to represent my school in an exchange program in Nigeria, Africa. After a year in Africa, I returned to college and fell in love with a young lady who I expected would become my wife.

I graduated in the spring of 1983 with all of my dreams and more accomplished! I had graduated with a degree in psychology and also managed to pick up a second degree in religion. I had visited another culture in Nigeria, Africa and even had the opportunity to visit seven other countries in Europe. And I had found the lady who I expected to become my wife.

I then found myself in trouble. I had accomplished all of my goals. What was I to do next?

With all my worldly possessions loaded down in a 10 year old Dodge Colt, I limped my way to Louisville, Kentucky in the fall of 1984. There were 2 reasons for this migration. One, I could go to school while I tried to figure out what I was supposed to do with my life. Second, the girl I had been dating for 2 years was graduating in the spring and planned to move to Louisville so she and I could see if our relationship would indeed move toward marriage.

Then it happened. I call it the flood. You remember the flood. That's when the water rises so fast you can't keep up and it destroys everything.

In the second week of October, I received a letter from my father which said he and my mother had gone to court to finalize a divorce which had been brewing for several years. This was devastating for me because I grew up in a great Christian home with a great relationship with my mother and a confidant type relationship with my father. I called that evening to learn that indeed it was true. I also learned that my father had filed for bankruptcy. Two days later he had a nervous breakdown.

With my family falling apart I realized I was in very serious trouble. While in school, I had been moving every 3 to 9 months for the past five years straight. In an effort to continue my education, I had come to Louisville, and like most students, I landed in Louisville with no job, no family, no church, no friends and no organizations that knew me.

My finances were pretty bleak as well. I had to take out a loan just to fund my living expenses.

On that Friday, I called the one thing I did have left in my life, the girl I intended to marry, who was still back at college. As soon as she answered the phone, I knew something was wrong. The sum of our conversation was that she had been in the arms of another man for 3 days. This was more than I could take. I felt like jumping out of the third story window I was standing near. It had been a rough week.

A few days later, I developed some minor physical problems, and you can guess what happened to my grades. During this mess, someone at school asked me "how are you doing?" I hesitated for a moment because I didn't know. Having a degree in psychology, I knew this hesitation and the realization that I didn't know 'how I was doing' was a problem. So, I sought out a counselor.

As bad as this sounds, it got worse. In February, I moved back to Cincinnati to help my father put his business back together. That was a mistake. All the anger and frustration my father felt due to his problems he turned against those closest to him, including me. This breach of our friendship was to change our relationship forever.

I tell this story for two reasons. First, I want you to know that I am an Anonymous American who started with nothing and who has faced trouble and difficulty. Second, I know many of you reading this book have been through similar situations. Your flood might have been being fired, going bankrupt, losing a child or going through a divorce. Someone reading this book may be going through a situation like this right now. I want you to know that you are not alone. All of us, including this motivational speaker, have been there. We survived and so will you.

In April of that year, a friend from Tokyo, Japan whom I had met through my college YMCA work, wrote and asked me to come to Japan and teach English. This was my way out of the flood.

While in Japan, a friend handed me a tape by Dr. Robert Schuller. In that tape, Dr. Schuller asked the question, "If the world were perfect, if you had all the time in the world, all the money in the world, **if you knew you could not fail, what would you do?**"

I thought "Well, I may not have anything else in my life, but at least I can still dream!" So, I took a clear file notebook and began to record all the things I would do if I knew I could not fail. Here is a partial list of the dreams I listed:

1. I want to have a perfect body. 160 pounds, sleeping 7 hours a day and ready to pass the Air Force fitness test.
2. I want the perfect personality. I listed all the characteristics that I wanted: loving, kind, tender, friendly, etc.
3. I want to get married and have a great family.
4. I want to have a successful sales career.
5. I want to own $250,000 worth of real estate.
6. I want to own 100 acres of land one hour from my home. This would be something I could play on, as well as pass along to my children and grandchildren, and it would also be a way to help preserve nature and wildlife by providing them a habitat.

I then began to formulate a big dream. I took the fruits of my psychology and religious education and began to write down the formation of a non-profit organization that would make a real difference in this world. I would call this organization the Creative Difference because our goal and mission is to create a positive difference in this world.

My goal with the Creative Difference would be to form businesses that would employ people, provide services and pay taxes. Then we could take the profits from those businesses and put them into permanent endowments. These endowments when invested would generate money we could then use once a year to help people through organizations like the Red Cross, Habitat for Humanity and the Nature Conservancy.

Now I want to ask you, am I a dreamer or am I a dreamer? I was in Japan for one year and I spent much of that time working on this master plan for my life. It is important to note here that I did not simply make a one page list of dreams like I have included here. What I did was to take a notebook and write a very detailed description of every dream I have ever had. This notebook was 1/2 inch thick. It contained pictures, charts and floor plans of my home. I came back to America and settled in Louisville, Kentucky ready to begin following my dreams.

During the next six years, following the techniques presented in this book, I developed a successful sales career as a stockbroker and financial planner in the Louisville area. I met, dated and married a beautiful young lady from my church, and we have a marvelous life together. We put together a portfolio of real estate that includes a 110 acre nature preserve within an hour drive from our home. The total value of our real estate holdings extends well over the quarter of a million dollar mark. I have also had the opportunity to start my own speaking business. All of this was accomplished by the time I was 32 years of age.

I consider myself an Anonymous American who started with nothing and who has been able to make my dreams come true. The great news is what I have done you can do! It all starts with your dream!

"If you can dream it, you can do it. Always remember that this whole thing was started with a dream and a mouse."

Walt Disney

Chapter 3

It all Started with a Dream!

Amber is a beautiful little girl with auburn hair and big blue eyes. As her uncle, it has been my pleasure and delight to watch her grow up. One evening when Amber was about 3 years old, I was over visiting her family. As the evening wore on, Amber fell asleep on the couch and my sister asked me to carry her up and put her into bed.

I slid my right arm under her neck and my left arm under her knees, lifted her up and gingerly started up the stairs. Halfway up the stairs Amber woke up slightly and asked, "Is it time to go to bed?"

"Yes," I responded.

As we got to her bed, I pulled back the covers and slid her legs under the covers and eased her head back on the pillow. I pulled the covers up around her neck to tuck her in.

Amber woke up and said, "Uncle Commie" (That's the best she could do with my name at 3 years of age.)

"Yes, Amber," I responded.

"I'm ready."

"You're ready? What are you ready for?"

"I'm ready to... dream again!"

That struck me like a bolt of lightning. "I'm ready to dream again." If there is anything we as people need, it is the ability to dream again.

We need to dream again because too many of us have had our dreams stolen. Too many people are walking around with broken, defeated and lifeless lives. They lack challenge, excitement, passion and motivation to live.

Have you had your dream stolen? It is easy to have your dreams stolen today. The news media constantly bombard us with put downs of people and their abilities. The constant reporting of drugs, crime, mass murder and corruption is designed to steal hope and our ability to dream.

This has gotten so bad that a woman came up to me the other day and told me she thought the people in Russia had more opportunities than we do here in the United States. She was very serious. Based on my recent trip to Russia, though, I had not reached the same conclusion. (Between the Mafia and government corruption, the Russian people are having trouble making progress toward democracy and a free market economy.) There are opportunities all over the world, but no one has the opportunities we have here in America.

There are others who want to steal our dreams, such as people who have tried and failed in their own lives, peers who don't want us to get ahead of them, and parents and people in authority who don't want us to try anything new. Even our so-called friends quite often want to keep us down on their level. All these people work very hard to steal our dreams.

I am convinced that no matter where you are in life, the answer to the dilemma of where you are and where you want to be is in your ability to dream again.

So, are you a college student wondering which career path you should follow? It's time to dream again!

Are you one of the thousands of people who have been displaced by this shifting economy either through termination or downsizing? It's time to dream again!

Are you a retired person wondering what you should do with the next 30 years of your life? It's time to dream again!

Are you doing OK with your career and family, but you are bored out of your mind? You seem to have hit a dull spot, things are OK, but just not exciting? Even though you may be doing OK it's time to dream again!

Despite all the negative press, dreams can still come true in this country! Just ask Debbie.

Debbie was a 20-year-old just barely out of high school, with no college education, no business experience and absolutely no money. (What is your problem?) However, Debbie had a dream! Her dream was to start a fastfood type restaurant that sold nothing but cookies.

In fact, if the truth be known, all Debbie had was her dream. Remember, she had no money, no college education, no business education, no business experience, she was barely 20 years old and had never sold anything in her life. And this is the lady who wanted to open a store front restaurant that sold nothing but cookies. Oh, she did have a great recipe for chocolate chip cookies, but that is hardly enough credentials for starting a new business.

But this would not stop Debbie. Armed with her cookies and her dream, Debbie went to banker after banker giving them some sample cookies and asking for start up money for her first store. The bankers would say, "How can a 20-year-old coed, or anyone for that matter, start a new type of retail store with no experience, no education and no money?" One by one every banker turned her down.

But Debbie would not stop. She noticed one interesting fact that gave her hope. Every banker who turned her down, also ate every bite of the sample cookies she gave them.

Eventually, Debbie found one person who believed in her dream and helped her establish her first store. Debbie insured the success of her great chocolate chip recipe by keeping her standards very high. She insisted on only the best ingredients and instructed her staff to never keep cookies on the shelf more than two hours.

And guess what happened? Everyone loved the cookies! They bought them by the dozen for the office and for parties. The cookies and the concept of a "cookie store" took off! That young lady is Debbie Fields of Mrs. Fields cookies. Today Mrs. Fields Cookies has over 800 stores world wide including the United Kingdom and Japan. Dreams can still come true in this country!

Like Debbie, you will face obstacles and people who will try to squelch your dream. But like Debbie, you can rise above those obstacles and follow your dreams.

Dreams give us life. They provide a hope for the future. A recent study conducted by the University of Southern California on aging found two distinct psychological reasons why people die. First they stop reading. That is, they stop learning and growing. Second, they stop believing things are possible. They stop dreaming. When we as people begin to get cynical and stop believing that new things are possible, we begin to die.

Dreams are simply desires placed into the future in the form of goals. They give us a reason to get up in the morning and purpose for our actions. It is this purpose for living; this passion for life that makes life worth living.

I love the way Walt Disney said it, "If you can dream it, you can do it. Always remember that this whole thing was started with a dream and a mouse." He is so right. I also love the quote from Tony Robbins who said, "If anyone can do anything in the world, you can too." He is right! If Walt Disney's dreams can come true, if Debbie Fields' dream can come true, if Conway Stone's dreams can come true, your dreams can also come true!

So, are you ready? Are you ready to dream again?

"Dreaming is an act of pure imagination, attesting in all people a creative power, which if it were available in waking would make every man a Dante or Shakespeare."

H. F. Hedge

Chapter 4
What is a Dream?

Quite simply a dream can be anything you want it to be. Dreams can be simple like learning to play a game or building a set of building blocks for your children.

I once had a dream of building a set of boxes in which I could plant strawberries. I wanted my wife to be able to raise the back window, lean out and pick a handful of strawberries for our supper. (As you can tell I dream big.)

The first half of that dream did come true. I built the boxes and planted the strawberries. The second half of that dream, the part about my wife leaning out the window and picking strawberries for our supper; well, let's just say we're still working on that one. The point is a dream can be anything.

One of my favorite stories to prove a dream can be anything is of Nigel Bryan of Australia. Nigel decided he wanted to get into the Guinness Book of Records by delivering the world's longest speech.

The rules were strenuous. He could use no reference material, could only take short rest breaks and had to talk continuously. At least 10 people had to be present for the entire record setting speech.

Nigel spoke on 50 topics ranging from world wide banking to aircraft repair. He even participated in a debate playing all 6 roles. When it was all said and done, Nigel made the Guinness Book of records by speaking for 50 hours and 40 minutes. (And you thought your boss spoke a long time.) This just goes to prove a dream can be anything.

Nigel's advice to you and me..."Anything worth having is worth the hard work required to achieve it."

Just to prove a dream can be anything, a friend of mine handed me a card with seven 4's on it. It became a dream of mine to arrange these 4's so they total 100. See if you can do it.

$$4 \quad 4 \quad 4$$

$$4 \quad 4 \quad 4 \quad 4$$

Answer: Place two sets of 4's side by side. 44 & 44. When you add these two numbers together you get 88. The remaining 4's are added together and you get 12. 88+12=100

Dreams can be much larger!

Dreams can be much larger like buying a new car or building a house. Ed Fackler of Harrison County, Indiana has a big dream. Ed is trying to find the perfect apple tree for the Ohio Valley. With apple production in Kentucky and Indiana alone topping 100 million pounds a year, Ed Fackler may have a gold mine if he is able to accomplish his dream of finding the perfect apple.

On his Rocky Meadow Orchard near Salisbury, Indiana, Ed had as many as 800 varieties of apple trees. One by one he has eliminated the varieties until today he has 470 varieties.

In his own words, "The tree must be easy to grow, easy to take care of and have an excellent taste. I may never find the ultimate apple tree for the Ohio Valley, but I like the challenge. I'm working on something I really love. I'm doing what I want with my life and I'm enjoying every minute of it!"

Dreams can be complex

Dreams can be complex like trying to start a business or an organization. Jim Baker of Victoria, Texas was getting fed up with the mutual funds in which he invested. Their fees were too high and they invested in companies he knew nothing about.

The solution? Start your own mutual fund, of course. Jim looked at his assets. First, he was an accountant. Second, he had been studying the market for years. Third, he had a client list of people who might be willing to invest.

Although the process was long and hard, Jim finally filed with the SEC and now heads the Am Trust Value Fund in Victoria, Texas. His fund has a 1% management fee. He invests in "common stocks of small to mid-size companies in the United States preferably in and around the Victoria, Texas area. Companies will be selected based on their value and capital appreciation."

Jim reminds me of one of my father's old sayings, "You are more than you think you are."

So we see that dreams can be anything you want them to be. They may be simple, large or complex. Anything can be a dream.

Why are you here?

But the question I want to ask is much deeper. Although the material in this book can be applied to any dream from an apple tree to learning how to speak well in front of others, the question I really want to ask is 'why are you here?' What is the reason you were placed here on this earth?

Bill Cosby, in one of his famous comedy sketches, talks about the worst thing you can hear your doctor say. When you are on the operating table, the last thing you want the doctor to say is "Ooops."

I have news for you. No one said "OOOPS" when you were born. God did not make a mistake. There is a reason why you are here. And the best way to self-fulfillment, the best way to happiness, is to get in touch with that reason and to align your actions and habits with that purpose.

Although all the people we have mentioned so far are good examples of people who have found the reason they are here, another good example is Yul Brenner. Yul Brenner played the king in the "King and I" for several years before he quit the production to pursue other interests.

A couple of years later, he rejoined the cast of the "King and I." When Johnny Carson asked him why he returned to the production, he responded, "This is what I am supposed to do." And if you ever saw that production, you know Yul Brenner was made for that role in the "King and I." He was a man at peace with himself and in touch with why he was placed here on this earth.

Why are you here? What are you supposed to be doing? What is your purpose and role here on earth? What is that dream you always wanted to accomplish? What is that goal you always thought you would like to do? What is that nagging idea you feel would really make this world better if someone would just do it?

Over the years people have called this 'reason for being' several different things.

- Some people call it the "inner voice."
- Others call it the "inner consciousness."
- Some people call it the "reason you are here."
- Still others call it the "inner self."
- If you are a Christian, you might call it "God's will for your life."
- If you are a star trek fan, you might call it "your destiny."
- If you are from the 60's, you might call it "your thing."
- If you are a new age person, you might call it "your self awareness."

No matter what you call it, there is a reason you were born and there are some dreams for you to accomplish.

One of the best ways to discover this purpose is to look at your dreams. What would you like to do? **Follow those dreams; they tell you who you are and why you are here on this earth.**

Oliver Wendell Holmes once said, "The tragedy of life is that too many of us die with our music still unplayed." This book is written so you will not take your music, your dreams and the reason you were placed here on earth to your grave. We need you as an Anonymous American to follow your dreams and have your music played.

Rosita Perez, a professional speaker friend of mine, puts it this way, "Are you singing the song you were sent to sing?"

The Definition of a Dream

You may be asking yourself, "this is all fine and good, but what is my dream? How do I know if I am living the music I was sent here to play?" Well, those questions can be answered by my definition of a dream.

My definition of a dream is this: **If the world were perfect, if you had all the money in the world and all the time in the world and you knew you could not fail, what would you do?**

That is the question Walt Disney answered when he dreamed of a place where families could come and spend the whole day. By answering the question 'what would I do if I knew I could not fail,' Walt Disney dreamed of Disneyland. And think of all the people who have enjoyed his dream. Think of all the smiles he has brought to families and all the employment he has provided. He was a man in touch with his dreams and the reason he was placed here on earth.

Take a moment and answer the question, "What would you do if you knew you could not fail?" List as many dreams as possible...

_____

_____

_____

_____

_____

_____

_____

FOLLOW YOUR DREAMS

WHAT WOULD YOU DO IF YOU KNEW YOU COULD NOT FAIL?

1 _____

2 _____

3 _____

Write three dreams you would like to accomplish.

"Dreams are a reflection of what you value and believe."

Rich Wilkins

Chapter 5
Where do Dreams come From?

Where do dreams come from? When I ask that question in my seminars and motivational presentations, I receive a number of interesting responses, such as: "Dreams come from the imagination. Dreams are something you dream up, desire or hope for." But where do dreams come from?

Dreams are not something you pull out of your imagination. They are not a wild fantasy. **Dreams are a reflection of what you value and believe.** [1]

Dreams

Values
&
Beliefs

Quite simply, if you value health and living a long time, you will have a dream of getting and staying in shape. If you value success, self-fulfillment, and money, you will dream of having a good job and working hard at that job. If you value relationships, you will dream of getting married and raising a close family. If you value excitement and seeing new things, you will dream of traveling and adventurous vacations. If you believe in God, you will dream of having a deep spiritual life.

[1] I owe a deep debt of gratitude to Rich Wilkins for the initiation of this model. For further information read, *Going Beyond a Positive Mental Attitude* by Rich Wilkins. 1-800-944-7269

As we can see, our values and beliefs are essentially who we are, because we act and behave based on what we believe and value. (You could substitute the words "care about" for value.) Our dreams are an outgrowth of those beliefs and values. That is why I say **follow your dreams; they tell you who you are.**[2]

How are beliefs and values formed?

Beliefs and values are formed by our continual thinking. By examining what we believe, by examining what we want to base our lives on, and by continually thinking about these beliefs, our beliefs and values are shaped.

The problem is many people never take the time to think through what they believe and value. And since they do not think about their beliefs and values, guess how their values are formed. **By accident!**

By this I mean most people buy what they value from the culture in which they grew up. They buy the beliefs of their parents, teachers, friends and books they read.

Is it any wonder we have trouble dreaming? If our dreams are an outgrowth of our beliefs and values, and if we have trouble knowing who we are because of a lack of thinking about what we believe and value, how can our dreams flow from these values? Is it any wonder that our dreams are muddled and unclear?

It is only when we question the beliefs and values of our society and then ask, "What do I believe? What do I know to be true?" that we begin to form and shape our own beliefs. It is then that our dreams can flow easily and become clear.

Let me give you two quick examples. For several years, I worked as a financial planner and stockbroker. While in this business, I was constantly amazed at the people who would invest in a stock or in an insurance company not because of their investigation and thought about these companies, but because of what their

[2] Although many psychologists and philosophers have stated that we act on what we believe, psychologist Albert Ellis is one of the early thinkers in this matter. Albert Ellis, Human Psychotherapy: the Rational-Emotive Approach, Chapter One. (New York: Julian Press, 1973)

brother-in-law had said about the company or because they heard a tip down at the local barber shop.

Having lived most of my life in Arkansas and Kentucky (states known for solid democratic voting), I am amazed at the people who voted straight democratic tickets without thinking why they did this. In fact when asked why, many would tell me, "because my father always voted that way." This is just another example of people buying into the values given to them by their parents rather than deciding for themselves.

If we have bought our political and financial values from other people, what else have we bought from them? Have we bought our spiritual values from others? Have we formed our opinion about our self-worth from other people? Have we figured out how many children we will have from the norms of our society?

The answer to living life by accident is to examine our beliefs and values and live our lives intentionally. Socrates put it best when he said, "The unexamined life is not worth living."

Many of us after having gone through the process of thinking about our beliefs and values have come back to believe and hold many of those values held and taught by our parents, church and society. But they become ours when we explore them for ourselves and not merely accept the teachings of our traditions.

Dreams

↑

Beliefs
&
Values

↑

Thinking

I have composed a series of questions designed to help you explore and think about what you believe and what you value. This is not designed to be the complete process for understanding yourself; it is simply designed to get you started in the process of thinking about what you value and believe. Answer each question as slowly and completely as you can.

1. Write a success list. Over the next two days complete a list of everything you have accomplished in your life. Simple things like completing high school. Complicated things like being a good parent or starting a business.

We do what we value. So looking at the things you have done is a great way to understand what it is you value.

2. What would you do if you knew you could not fail? If there were no limitations, such as time, money or circumstances, what would you do? Write those dreams down in as much detail as possible. Our dreams are an outgrowth of our beliefs and values; by answering this question we get an indication of what it is we care about.

3. What are the principles you have built your life on? If you were shipped to a foreign country and everything you had been taught was proven to be false, what would you still believe? If you had to develop a series of universal principles that everyone in this world had to hold true, what would they be?

This can be a very hard question. Yet, it is very real. I had to face it.

I grew up in a small-town Southern Baptist culture of northeast Arkansas. I had a thousand rules that I lived by and felt the rest of the world should live by. Some of those rules were: no drinking, no cussing, no smoking, no dancing. Then, while in college, I had the good fortune to live in Nigeria, Africa as an exchange student for one year. Was I ever in for a surprise!

In the Nigerian culture, dancing was a way of life, just like breathing or eating. I could not believe this. My little set of rules that had been closely crafted since I was 3 years old was destroyed. It got worse.

I met missionaries who cussed occasionally and were still very spiritual people. They did a great deal of work for the kingdom of God. I met other missionaries from Europe who scoffed at the idea of never taking a drink.

I had to come to terms with the fact that the rules I had grown up with did not work in this foreign culture. As I sat down to think about this, I threw away all the rules I had been taught all my life and started with a clean sheet of paper. My goal was to develop five universal principles I could believe and hold true no matter what happens. What would still be true, no matter what culture I went to or even if we found life on other planets? This was the question I was trying to answer.

I would like to offer to you here the 5 principles I developed to live my life by. I offer these principles as a backdrop for you; to let you see my thinking and what I believe. I will also ask you to explore your own values. What do you believe would be true no matter what happens?

1. God is the creator of all.
    1a) When I have found love or truth, I have found God.
    1b) Truth will eventually win out.
    1c) Illusion is evil's greatest weapon.

2. The meaning of life is to love God.

3. Everyone is my superior in that I may learn from them.

4. Nothing is wrong in and of itself. It is our abuse of it that makes it wrong.

5. Creativity and positive expectation can affect the outcome of any situation. [3]

These are the principles I have built my life upon. What would be the principles that you will build your life upon?

---

[3] I have developed an entire presentation based on these principles, called "Steps along the Journey." You can order this series by calling 1-888-899-5353

4. What epitaph would you want on your tombstone? This can be a compelling question to ponder. What is the final phrase you would like spoken for you? I hope everyone at my grave would be able to say, "He made a difference."

5. If a fire were coming and you could only get three things out of your house...what would they be?

6. If you had 6 months to prepare a lecture and deliver it as if it were the final words you would ever say to your family and friends...what would you say?

7. If you were to build the perfect business, organization, church or country, what would it look like? What kind of work would it do? How would it function? How would people treat one another? What kind of people would you hire?

8. When you are 90 years old, sitting in a rocking chair and looking back over your life, **is there anything you would regret not doing?** For example, if you did not get an MBA would you regret that? Would you regret not having learned to fly? Follow those desires and urges. Those are dreams that can make life fulfilling.

9. Write a list of 100 things you would like to do before you die. Lou Holtz used this method after a near plane crash in 1969. He broke his goals into 5 sections; personal, professional, financial, travel and interesting things to do. Two of his goals on that list were to coach football at the University of Notre Dame and to win a national championship. He has accomplished both of those goals as well as most of his other goals. This type of list will give you an indication of what you care about.

These questions are designed to get you started thinking about the beliefs and values you hold. This thinking process is necessary to move beyond the values given us by our parents to our own values.

Finding out what you really believe and value may require more than just thinking. Once you get your values listed, it is now time to experience them. Values are easy on paper. It is another thing to live them and experience them in relationships, families and at work.

Thinking about your dreams, values and beliefs takes effort. But it is some of the most valuable work of life because it is from our values that our dreams come. I would not take anything for my year in Nigeria where I came to terms with the 5 principles on which I have based my life and work. It is out of these beliefs that I have been able to dream and dream big.

*"My life seems to be one long obstacle course
with the chief obstacle being me."*

Jack Parr

Chapter 6

Why People do not Follow Their Dreams!

Why do people not follow their dreams? That is a very good question. Take a moment and list the reasons why the people you know do not follow their dreams.

1.   6.

2.   7.

3.   8.

4.   9.

5.   10.

Now list reasons why you do not follow your dreams. Perhaps there are some personal reasons why you do not follow your dreams.

1.

2.

3.

4.

Bobby Knight, the famous basketball coach at Indiana University who has won 3 NCAA championships, once said, "If you want to succeed, list the things that stop you from succeeding. Then one by one overcome those obstacles and you will succeed."

Taking this advice, I took a couple of days and listed all the things that were blocking my progress toward my goals. I was doing a mass mailing and I kept a legal pad on the table as I stuffed envelopes. Every time an idea came to mind, I would pause and write it down.

I was astonished to find 53 obstacles to my progress. It took 7 legal size pages to write down all the obstacles in my way. This was a very revealing and valuable exercise for me.

Would this be a valuable exercise for you? List 6 habits or obstacles that are preventing you from accomplishing your dreams.

1.   4.

2.   5.

3.   6.

Let's look at a few of the most common reasons why people do not follow their dreams. These are some of the most common responses gathered from my presentations and seminars:

1. Fear of Failure. This is usually the first thing people mention. In fact the fear of failure grips everyone from time to time. The thoughts come rapidly, "What would happen if I failed? What would happen if it doesn't work out? What would happen if people do not buy? What if? What if? What if? How would I appear to my family and friends if I do not make it?"

For me, overcoming the fear of failure has become easier by accepting three facts. **#1 Life is hard.** Life is so hard that no matter what you attempt, you are going to face problems, setbacks and difficulties. Once we accept this fact, facing our fear is much easier, because we know that setbacks are going to come, but they do not mean we have failed. We can look at them as mere obstacles and steps in our way to succeeding.

Excuse the simple example, but how many times does a baby fall in learning to walk? No one would ever accuse a baby of failing simply because they fall while learning to walk. We know that falling is simply part of the process of learning to walk. The same is true of following our dreams. Sometimes we will fall, but that is part of the process of learning to walk.

Why then are we so hard on the colleague or family member who makes a mistake in learning something new? Why are we so hard on the boss whose new idea doesn't work well? Why are we so hard on ourselves? Life is hard and the setbacks are not necessarily failures; they are just stepping stones to being successful. As you know babies do learn to walk. I like the way Debbie Fields says it, "The surest way to fail is to not try."

#2 We all fail. Not all of our goals and plans turn out the way we had planned. Everyone fails but this should not stop us. We can still follow our dreams. Accepting this fact makes it easier to deal with failure.

Dr. Robert Schuller is fond of saying, "I'd rather see a crooked furrow than an unplowed field."

#3 Failure is a part of success. Many times we know we are making progress by the number of problems stopping us from following our dreams. Sometimes life does not want us to accomplish. So, we have a lot of obstacles in our way to prevent us from doing something. Some famous people in history have known they were doing the right thing by the number of people who tried to stop them. Again, a quote from Dr. Robert Schuller, "I'd rather try and fail than to do nothing and succeed."

Many times fear of failure is actually fear of the unknown. You don't know what will happen if you fail. I have found two solutions to this fear.

#1 List out all the possible outcomes. Be creative. List the worst possible outcome of the situation. List the bizarre possibilities. If you can live with the worst possible outcome, you can live with any other outcome.

If the worst were to happen, how bad could it be? I could lose my money, or the time I put into that project. I could look foolish. In my experience the actual outcome is usually not as bad as my worst case scenario. This exercise may take away the fear of the unknown.

#2 Face the fear. Mark Twain once said, "90% of my fears never occurred." This is so true. Many times the fears we face are from our own imagination and will never happen. Go ahead and face the fear, do the action. Many times the fear is not real. It's not there at all.

2. Another fear that grips many people is the fear of success. If I try and succeed, then who and what I am will change. If I start my own business, I will be away from my family and friends more. If I am successful, I will have to change my lifestyle and live differently than I currently do. This fear prevents people from moving ahead and achieving.

Many of us have been taught that money is evil. And thus succeeding would be bad. Therefore not trying becomes the easiest way to comply with that thinking.

3. Time is a factor that stops many people. One of the biggest cries we hear today is, "I don't have enough time." And the truth is we do have a lot of pressure on our time with jobs, family, children and other obligations.

But here is a truth we seem to forget. We have all the time there is. Each of us has 24 hours a day. This has not changed since the history of the world. In truth, we have more time than most people in history have had because our expected life span is longer than any generation in recorded history.

If our lives are too busy, then maybe we need to eliminate some of the things in our lives that cause us to be so busy. Maybe we need to say "NO" to things that do not help us reach our dreams.

If our lives are still too busy, then maybe there are things in our lives that are more important than our dreams. Maybe we really don't want to follow our dreams if we keep allowing other things to get in the way.

Thank God time did not stop Thomas Edison, Thomas

Jefferson, George Washington and other dreamers. They accomplished their dreams and so can we.

4. Habits. Many of us have habits that are not conducive to following our dreams. Psychologists tell us we have pictures in our heads of how we believe things ought to be. These pictures have been formed over all of our lives, but especially during our childhood. For the most part, our lives are mirrors of those pictures. Our habits are what allow us to continue living according to these pictures.[4]

Old habits or patterns of living can cause us to live very unhealthy lives. To overcome these habits and bad patterns of living, we must put new habits, ideas and pictures in our minds. This is done most effectively with affirmations and anchors. These will be discussed later in this book.

5. Money. This is an age old excuse. Let me state this clearly: **No Dreamer has ever had enough money to accomplish their dreams.** Col. Sanders started with a $90 social security check. Walt Disney was bankrupt when he started talking to people about the concept of Mickey the Mouse. These men have proven that dreams can come true even without money.

It's funny to note that even billionaires like Donald Trump have to borrow money to implement their dreams.

There are 1,000 other excuses: I'm lazy, I'm too old, I'm too young, my circumstances prevent success, people around me make success impossible. **But let me ask a serious question, are any of these excuses worth exchanging your dreams for?** Follow your dream in spite of the problems.

My Story

Do you remember my story of devastation? Do you think I faced those problems that stop most people from following their

---

[4] Although a number of psychologists talk about habits and how they affect our lives, William James, a philosopher and psychologist, was one of the first to document the power of habits. He referred to habits as "the enormous fly-wheel of society." William James, *Principles of Psychology*, 2 vols., Henry Holt and Co., New York, 1890.

dreams? I could not see straight. I had no money, no job, no friends, my family had fallen apart. I had all kinds of fear, bad habits, bad circumstances, no money, poor health and poor time management. But I would not quit!

No matter where you are, you can still dream. The circumstances and fears of your life are not worth giving up your dreams for. Don't let anyone steal your dream!

Why Small Businesses Fail

Michael Gerber is the founder of the Gerber Business Development Corporation and the author of the E-Myth. He has compiled a list of 10 reasons why small businesses fail. If your dream is to start a business, perhaps this will help you.

1. Lack of management systems. Many entrepreneurs have no systematic way of getting and using information.
2. Lack of vision.
3. Lack of financial planning and review.
4. Overdependence on specific individuals or suppliers in the business.
5. Poor market segmentation or strategy. Many entrepreneurs don't know who their customers are. Factors include age, location, and why they buy.
6. Failure to establish or communicate company goals.
7. Lack of knowledge about their competition.
8. Inadequate capitalization. It is easy to start a business but often very hard to stay in business.
9. Absence of standardized quality programs. 'How can we get better?' is a constant question.
10. Owners concentrate on the technical rather than the strategic work at hand. It is easier to do a simple job than to think about the future.

UNLOCKING OBSTACLES TO YOUR DREAMS

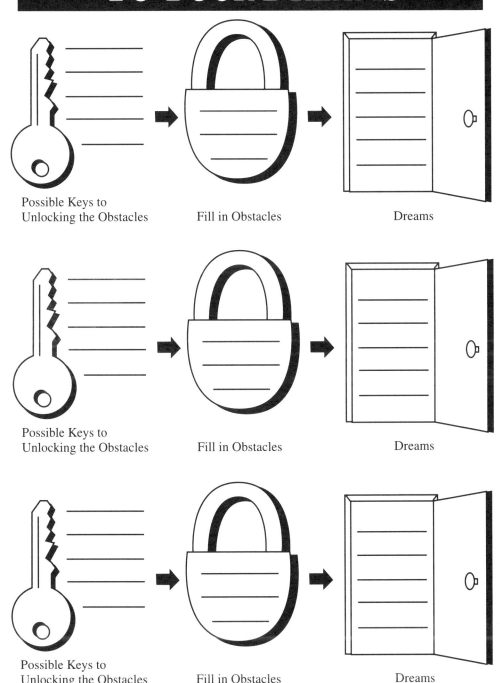

Possible Keys to
Unlocking the Obstacles

Fill in Obstacles

Dreams

Possible Keys to
Unlocking the Obstacles

Fill in Obstacles

Dreams

Possible Keys to
Unlocking the Obstacles

Fill in Obstacles

Dreams

"*Most men die from the neck up by the age of 25, because they stop dreaming.*"

Ben Franklin

Chapter 7

Is There a Cost in not Following Your Dream?

You have heard the phrase, dreams are free. That is true, but following your dreams is not free. There is a price to pay. For example, Col. Sanders took his chicken recipe to 1,000 restaurant owners before the first restaurant owner decided to buy his chicken recipe. It cost him months of his life to follow his dreams. Jonas Salk spent his life in search for a cure for polio and other diseases. It cost John Kennedy and Abraham Lincoln their lives to follow their dreams for this country.

There is an old story told of George Washington. After the long battle for the freedom of the United States and after a long battle to obtain a constitution, there came a time of crisis. It seems that the military leaders had felt the country was going in the wrong direction and they were having a meeting deciding if they should oppose the civilian leadership of the country. George Washington heard rumors of their meeting and decided to go address the troops. In a very passionate speech, Washington encouraged the men to stay loyal to the country and it's constitution. Then he pulled out a document to read, and after a few seconds he had to reach in his pocket for a pair of glasses. His words to the men were, "Gentlemen, as you can see I have given my eyesight for this great country." It cost George Washington the prime of his life and his eyesight to establish this country. Dreaming is easy. But there is a cost to following your dreams.

When I was in high school, I lived in the basement of our home. One evening my father came stomping down stairs yelling, "Conway, I'm going to write a book entitled, '**I Understand Women!**' It is going to have 475 blank pages!"

My father and I have laughed about that book at least twice a year for the past 22 years. Recently, I was in the local book store and I found a book entitled, "Everything Men Know about Women." The book is written by Dr. Alan Francis, a psychologist. It has a 4-star rating from the Times and an endorsement from the Chronicle. And you guessed it; it contains 127 blank pages!

Now the nut who put this book together is probably sitting on the beach somewhere in the Caribbean, enjoying the sun, while I'm still working my fool head off. I even paid him $3.00 for his book! It is costly to follow your dreams, but if you don't, someone might just do it for you.

I would like to tell you the story of my grandfather. When he found out I was in this business, he asked me to take a walk one day and he told me about opportunities in his life. He said, "Conway, when I was in Tokyo during World War II, I had a decent business going as a money exchanger. When I got back from the war, I could have taken that talent and become a banker, but I didn't. A couple of years later I asked a big shot millionaire in town if he would give me enough money to open a typewriter and office supply store in an empty storefront on main street. That millionaire said, 'No, I won't give you enough money to open a single store on main street, but I will loan you enough money to open 10 stores across the state of Arkansas.'" My grandfather went on to say, "Man, I jumped away from that, saying No! No! I just want to open one store, not 10.

"You know, son, a few years later after working on typewriters for years, I came up with an idea for an invention. I figured out how to make a manual typewriter return it's carriage automatically without electricity. The idea was worth millions as an invention, but I never pursued that idea.

"You see, I've had my chances, but I did not follow the dreams and the chances I had. And now as I sit drawing my pension and social security, I realize I could have done more.

"I'm telling you this as a grandfather, so you won't make the same mistakes I have made. I'm also telling you because you are in the position to tell others, **It costs a great deal to follow your dreams, but it costs even more not to follow your dreams.**"

With that, my grandfather patted me on the back and we walked back into the house. I knew I would never forget that moment and that I would do my best to pass on this wisdom from my grandfather.

Yes, it does cost a great deal to follow your dreams, but oh, the cost of not following your dreams! What would have happened if Jonas Salk had not followed his dream of finding a cure for polio? What would have happened if Thomas Edison had not had enough time to invent the light bulb? How many millions of smiles would we have lost if Walt Disney would have said, "I don't have any money; I can't do anything" and not followed his dream of building Disneyland? The cost to the world of these men not following their dreams would have been enormous. **It costs a great deal to follow your dreams, but it costs even more not to follow your dreams.**

A minister once said, "the most expensive real estate in the world is the cemetery, because too many ideas and dreams are buried there forever." Don't let this happen to you. Follow your dreams in spite of the problems.

"The only hope we have is for Anonymous Americans to get in touch with their beliefs and values and follow their God given dreams."

Conway Stone

Chapter 8

Dreamers: Our only Hope!

Why is all this important? Well, we have a lot of problems in this country with drugs, poverty, apathy, overpopulation, cynicism, divorce, teenage pregnancy, etc. Yet, these problems have not been solved by churches or by non-profit organizations (who take 30 to 50 percent of their contributions for administration) or by government agencies. The only hope we have is for Anonymous Americans to get in touch with their beliefs and values and follow their God given dreams, and solve these problems. You are our only hope!

Let me give you several examples:

Welfare is a major problem in this country. It has helped some people, but many people have gotten into the habit of receiving welfare checks and have stayed on welfare for generations. And despite its best efforts, the government has not been able to solve this problem. What is the answer? Anonymous Americans following their dreams is the only answer!

Do you know the name Peter Cove? Probably not because he is an Anonymous American. Peter founded a company called America Works. The mission of America Works is to take people who are on welfare, educate them, give them social interaction skills and training, and then help them find permanent work in the community.

The state of New York pays America Works $5,300 for each person they get off the welfare roles. So far, America Works has helped over 5,000 people get permanently off the welfare rolls.

The state of New York saves $17,000 every year for every person taken off welfare. And now the city of New York is looking to hire America Works to do the same thing for the city.

Where government fails, Anonymous Americans by following their dreams are succeeding.

Would you agree that the environment is a serious problem today? We are losing 4,000 acres of forests every day. This is significant for several reasons. First, we need the forests because they produce oxygen for people to breathe. Second, we need forests because they produce the moisture and perpetuate the precipitation cycles. Third, they provide a home for animals to roam and breed freely. The government has done a decent job of protecting land in government parks and forests, but the government cannot do it all. The parks are put under tremendous pressure to be used for timbering, oil production and development. If our wilderness lands are going to be preserved for animals and future generations, they are going to need our help.

There are a lot of organizations that talk about protecting forests. But if you look at them closely, they are more talk than they are action. They spend more money on administration and reports than they do on protecting land. So, what are we to do?

Enter an Anonymous American by the name of John Sawhill, who is president of the Nature Conservancy. Since 1951 this organization has taken donations from Anonymous Americans (like me) and bought land. Their purpose is to find the most fragile ecosystems in the world and protect them by buying the land and keeping it in trust for natural purposes.

Where ecology has become a recent fad in our culture, the Nature Conservancy has been acquiring land since 1951. They own 1,300 nature preserves in the United States and Canada. They have protected 7.5 million acres. They are heavily involved in the protection of rain forests in South America. Eighty-one percent of the donations goes to protect land.

Where government stops, Anonymous Americans following their dreams have found solutions and more importantly are implementing vibrant solutions.

Health care is a serious problem in this country. Although we have some of the best health care in the world, many people do not have access to our health care system, the chance of losing health care coverage is tremendous, and the cost is growing out of control. No one has a brilliant solution.

Enter Anonymous American Janice Guthrie. She grew up in Hope, Arkansas where, like most girls, she played hopscotch, went to school and attended Sunday School. After marriage and a couple of children, she got a job at the University of Arkansas earning $12,000 a year. And then at 39 she developed ovarian cancer. She was numb with panic when the doctors told her they wanted to operate as soon as possible.

To regain some control of her life, she went to the university library and painstakingly found the latest research on her form of cancer. After hours of research she had a stack of research 6 inches thick. The next time she sat down with her doctors, she knew as much as they did about the latest research of her type of cancer.

She had found that surgery and radiation did not keep people with her type of cancer alive any longer than just regular checkups. Her doctor sneered at her and her information. That made her mad.

Upon further research she also found a doctor in Houston, Texas who had successfully treated her type of cancer without surgery. Today she sports a clean bill of health.

And then she had a dream. **"I wonder if other people would benefit from this type of research..."** From the midst of her personal crisis, Janice Guthrie developed a company called Health Resources, Inc. of Little Rock, Arkansas. Health Resources started with Janice's dream of helping other people with her research. So she cleaned out her garage and started Health Resources with a $500 computer.

For approximately $250, she will gather the latest research on your particular disease and mail it to you. So, when you talk with your doctor, you will have the latest research on your disease.

Over the years Janice has helped 5,000 people and currently helps about 1,000 a year. This Anonymous American, by following her dream, has done more for the betterment of some people's health than all the politicians in Washington.

Hunger is a problem in this world. Although many people have tried, few have done more than keep a small number of people from starving for a little while. Giving away food helps people right now, but in the long run people need to learn how to grow and develop their own food. Programs by governments have provided limited success.

However, Anonymous American Jim Esdue of Waco, Texas is making a difference with this problem. As founder of World Hunger Inc., Jim has found a solution to world hunger in a self contained food system he has developed. With a handful of seeds, two rabbits and a special alfalfa tree, a family can grow enough food to prevent malnutrition for their family forever. Jim and his people have trained missionaries who have implemented this system throughout the world.

Let me conclude with one of my favorite stories. Millard Fuller, an Anonymous American from Atlanta, Georgia, has always had compassion for people who work in this country but who may never have the opportunity to own their own home. However, for years Millard ignored this compassion and pursued a business career. Although he became a millionaire, Millard was not happy. After a personal family crisis, Millard Fuller gave up his business pursuits and began to follow his dream of helping the working poor in this country to own their own homes.

This is a problem the government has tried to solve for years by building government housing. But when people move into housing they do not own, they turn those homes into government slums. Millard Fuller concluded that people who own their own homes maintain them better and they have a tendency to find work and to stay at their jobs longer. They usually vote and donate some time to a local charity.

So Millard Fuller began a organization called Habitat for Humanity. Habitat for Humanity takes applications from people who work, but who earn so little, they will never have the opportunity to own a home. Applicants' salaries are usually between $9,000 and $19,000.

Those chosen for a Habitat for Humanity home are required to put in 500 hours of work on their new home. Through the efforts of volunteers (everyone from retired people to working bankers, contractors and architects), Habitat for Humanity can build a modest three bedroom, one bath home for somewhere between $20,000 and $40,000. The house is then sold to the new owners with no money down and interest free payments for 20 years.

By one Anonymous American following his dream, thousands of families who would never have had a hope of owning a home, today have found the dignity and self worth in home ownership. And thousands of other people have found fulfillment by volunteering for Habitat for Humanity. Where the government has failed, one Anonymous American has succeeded.

In my opinion this is the only hope we have. If we are to overcome drugs, poverty, the health care crisis, welfare, guns in the street, overpopulation and apathy, just to name a few, it will not be because of governments, or churches or non-profit organizations who take 40 to 80 percent of their revenues for administration.
NO! It will be because of Anonymous Americans, people like you and me and Janice Guthrie and Millard Fuller, who by following their God given dreams have made a difference in this world.

So Anonymous Americans, **Follow your Dreams...You make a difference...You are the only hope we have.**

"There is nothing like a dream to create the future."

Victor Hugo

Chapter 9
What is your Dream?

So the question is this, **"WHAT IS YOUR DREAM?"** Why were you placed here on earth? It may be for something simple; to be a good parent or a good spouse. It may be for something great like starting an organization or building a business. Take your time. Explore all the possible things you would like to do, but answer this question, "If you had all the time in the world, all the money in the world and knew you could not fail; what would you do?"

Take a moment and write down the answer to that question. Here are some prompts to help you list your dreams. Provide as many details as possible.

My dream for my life is _____

_____

_____

My dream for my family is _____

_____

_____

My professional or business dream is _____

_____

_____

My health and wellness dream is _____

_____

_____

My financial dreams are _____

_____

_____

My spiritual dreams are _____

_____

_____

My dreams for friends, community, etc. are _____

_____

_____

My fun or outrageous dreams are _____

_____

_____

Remember, if Janice Guthrie, Debbie Fields and Conway Stone can follow their dreams and make them come true, you can too!

"Humanity cannot forget its dreamers. It cannot let their ideas fade and die. It lives in them. It knows them as the realities which it shall one day see and know. Composers, sculptors, painters, poets, prophets and sages; these are the makers of tomorrow. These are the architects of heaven."

John Donne

Chapter 10

People who have Followed their Dreams

I want to include here examples of people who have followed their dreams and are now making a difference in this world. I hope these stories will inspire you to follow your dreams as they have inspired me. I also hope these stories will trigger new ideas in your mind about dreams you can follow.

Some of these are famous people and others are Anonymous Americans. You will also notice that each of them has paid the price of following their dreams by overcoming problems and excuses.

1. When Col. Harlan Sanders was 65 years old, he received his first social security check for $90. He said, "I am not going to live like this." The Colonel also knew that many retired people who do not have both a reason to live and something to do, usually died very soon. So at the age of 65, Col. Harlan Sanders developed a reason to live in the form of a dream. He dreamed of opening a restaurant based on his wife's chicken recipe. He took his $90 social security check and his dream around the country. Tony Robbins likes to tell that Col. Sanders took that recipe and asked 1,000 people to buy his chicken recipe, before one person said yes. Today Kentucky Fried Chicken has become one of the most successful restaurant chains and franchises in the world. And the Colonel lived to a great old age.

Are you having trouble with persistence? Are you too old? The reason there is only one man named Col. is because of persistence. If he can start KFC at age 65, you can follow your dreams at your age.

Follow your dreams, in spite of your age.

2. Walt Disney was a dreamer. He dreamed of a place where families could go to have fun together. Many people do not know that Walt Disney was bankrupt when he went around the country showing his drawing of a mouse with a falsetto voice to bankers, investors and friends. There are a lot of steps from bankruptcy, to a dream, to Disneyland and the Walt Disney Corporation. Disney dreamed and worked on Disneyland for years before it became reality. His dream was a preview of his future.

If your dreams are a preview of your future, you will certainly want to dream big.

Follow your dreams, they are a preview of your future.

3. Sam Walton was a dreamer. Sam Walton dreamed of owning a national chain of value priced variety stores. His first variety store went bankrupt. His second variety store went bankrupt. But Sam knew that he could dream again. He knew that dreams are free and they provide hope for the future. Sam Walton persisted in his dream and formed the Wal Mart Corporation. Today the Wal Mart Corporation is one of the world's largest retailers.

Follow your dreams despite your financial problems.

4. Even idealists can make their dreams come true. Just take the case of David Marsh. David was a philosopher and a social worker with a passion for woodworking. How would you like to be a philosopher/social worker with a passion for woodworking and then try to make a living?

David decided to start a different type of woodworking business; a business that is more of a social experiment. He believed that people who enjoyed their work would produce the best products, and if you give people freedom, they will take pride in their work and do their best.

David hires artists who want to create works of art. They are free to experiment and create the most unique pieces of furniture. Much of their work is made on the simple styles of the Shakers and other folk styles.

In 1993, David Marsh's company sold $1.8 million worth of furniture in 20 states, Europe and Japan.

He tells his workers, "If it's not fun, don't do it. Joy and excitement in life are not an accident. They come by design; by the choices you make. What you do because you love it, is your best investment in yourself, and your best chance at success."

Let's hear it for an idealist who became a success by following his dream, who has helped 44 people live their dreams, and who has brought pleasure to thousands of people by following his dreams.

Follow your dreams even if they seem too idealistic.

5. Are you too old to "Follow your Dreams?" Do you believe that old dogs can't learn new tricks? Bernard Vonderschmitt, might prove you wrong. Vonderschmitt was an electrical engineer for RCA for 25 years. In 1979 he concluded that RCA had lost it's desire for cutting edge technology, so Vonderschmitt left the company.

What is a man to do at 56 years of age? Of course, go to college! Vonderschmitt enrolled in an MBA program.

Four years later, at the age of 60, Vonderschmitt with two other colleagues started a new company called Xilinx, Inc. Xilinx is a maker of customized computer chips. They make their computer chips at a fraction of the cost of the rest of the industry. Consequently, his company is very successful.

Today Vonderschmitt is in his eighties, is in good health and has no plans of stepping down. If he can do it **you can do it!** Age is no excuse.

6. Are your circumstances bad? Virginia Lewis had no money, no education, an abusive husband and two children to support.

The answer for Virginia was to buy a casino in Colorado. It took determination and all her experience as a cook and night manager. But with the research she had done in Las Vegas, Virginia's casino is making money. $7 million a year in fact. She is successful when half of the Colorado casinos are considered to be losing money.

Virginia's secret? Specialize. Her casino has decor, music and space for the "40 something" crowd.

7. Dennis was a national marketing director for Sony Corporation of America. His wife, Ann, was a freelance copywriter for Bloomingdale's and Macy's. Both were living in the fast lane and destined for bigger and better things. But they were tired of the rat race.

So in 1983 they quit the rat race and headed for Sandpoint, Idaho. This remote town in the middle of a natural wilderness sits on the shores of a 43 mile long lake. Ospreys and bald eagles fly overhead. If one looks carefully you can find grizzly bears and caribou in the nearby mountains.

So what are two yuppies going to do in a logging town, where the only employment is restaurants and discount stores? **Follow their Dreams of course!** These were not romantic idealists, but very practical successful business people who decided to live life their way. They started a mail order business.

As marketers they knew that having a specific product for a specific client was the key. Their target market was to be people like they used to be, yuppies stuck in pressure packed jobs and traffic of New York, L.A. and Chicago who would love to live and work in Yosemite but don't have the courage, skills or the time.

Gleaning names from magazines like the New Yorker and Audubon, the Pence's began to look for products that would appeal to their clients: nature related gifts from regional artists. Indian style earrings and belt buckles were their first orders.

Today their debt free company employs 80 people and grosses $18 million in sales. They live in a 4 bedroom home on 3 acres overlooking Lake Pend Oreille. Are you stuck in the rat race? If they can do it so can you!

8. Jacquetta Graham was an unemployed mother of 6, heavily in debt, separated from her husband and 40 years of age. In a mock job interview, Jackie kept insisting she wanted to go to school. This caught the attention of social worker Ken Evans of the Wesley Community House, where Jackie was staying and trying to get help. Mr. Evans mentioned her desire for an education in a meeting the next day and the director of Lindsey Wilson College agreed to give Jackie the chance to follow her dream of going to school.

Jackie's story has a message for all of us: You must grab the opportunity that comes your way. Jackie has completed 13 hours of university courses and sports a 4.0 grade point average. She dreams of becoming an accountant and is well on her way.

I love to tell the stories of the Anonymous Americans. Think about what Ken Evans has done for Jackie, her children and all the people Jackie will touch and help over the years. Because he is following his dreams this Anonymous American is making a difference in the lives of people.

And don't forget about the thousands of Methodists who over the years have contributed and supported the Lindsey Wilson College. In my opinion, these are the real heroes of this story.

9. Are you too old to follow your dreams? Mrs. Rose Blumkin of Omaha, Nebraska might prove you wrong. Born in Russia, Mrs. Blumkin came to this country in 1917 on a peanut ship. Mrs. B., as she is known around Omaha, worked hard and eventually owned and ran a $180 million carpet company.

At the age of 90 she sold her carpet company in an arrangement that allowed her to stay on and help run the business while her family retained 20% ownership. After a tiff with her grandson she quit the family business, announcing, "I never signed a no-compete clause." At the seasoned age of 95, she started another carpet business. She celebrated her 100th birthday on December 15, 1993, riding her wheelchair and running a $5 million carpet business. Her advice, "My daughters are retired; not me. I make my money the old fashioned way. I work very, very hard."

11. Larry Walters, a 33-year-old truck driver, dreamed of flying. But education and money were not the fate for Larry Walters; so his dream was postponed. One day while in his backyard, Larry found a way to realize his dream. He strapped 42 weather balloons to his lawn chair, grabbed his pellet gun and a six pack of beer and began to ascend into the air.

Larry and his applauding neighbors, expected he would rise about 400 to 500 feet. Wouldn't you have liked to have seen the faces when Larry rose 16,000 feet in the air floating right through the flight path of the L.A. international airport?

After a while, Larry took his pellet gun, shot out the weather balloons one at a time and slowly brought his chair to a soft landing.

If Larry Walters can accomplish a crazy dream like this, your dreams, too, can come true.

12. Lajos Nagy was a son of a minister in Balatonkiliti, Hungary. He went to Russia to study textiles and was a card carrying member of the Communist Party. Then Nagy had a dream of selling products to refugees. How would you like to start life with those types of credentials?

But Nagy continued with his dream. With a German partner, Nagy started making products for refugees. Items like tents, stoves, cots and cooking utensils. His clients include the United Nations, the International Red Cross and a half-dozen other national governments. In its fourth year in business, Balaton-Trade produced $5.7 million in revenues. This was an obvious need that many people had overlooked.

13. Mary Granderson lived in a small town in central Arkansas. As a Christian woman, she struggled with a way to live her faith with the people of her community. She taught Sunday School, vacation bible school, led the singing in her church, but this was not enough, she wanted to do more. She dreamed of taking her faith to the people outside of her church. Mary found her vehicle in Avon. As an Avon distributor, she could visit the homes

of people, even poor people in her community. When the sub-
ject of religion came up, she could simply share what she
believed about God.

Over the years I have noticed hundreds of people who get
ideas like this and try to make a difference in the world. But most
of them give up in just a few short months. Mary Granderson has
been visiting and helping the same families in her town for 25
years. This is the fulfillment of a dream that I admire.

The stories of people who have followed their dreams could
continue forever. I could tell you about famous people like Bill
Gates, Robert Schuller, and Lee Iacocca. I could tell you about
my personal heroes like Curt Brisco, Rich Wilkins and John
Claypool. But time won't permit. Those will have to wait for
another book.

It is my hope that these stories will serve to prove that people
who follow their dreams can overcome extraordinary odds. The
truth is if you and I can't make our dreams come true, who can?

We have as much time as anyone has ever had in the history of
the world. If you don't believe me, let me ask this question: Who
in the history of the world has ever had more than 24 hours a day?

We have more money than anyone has ever had in the history
of the world. Just check your salary with the salary of your parents
or grandparents. Check the buying power of your salary as com-
pared to that of your parents or grandparents.

We have more education and awareness than anyone has ever
had in the history of the world. With all the universities studying
minute details of virtually every aspect of our lives, we have access
to information and awareness on any detail of life.

Earl Nightingale was fond of saying that "all of history has worked
together to bring civilization to this point so that you and I can follow our dreams." We have the opportunity to follow and accomplish
our dreams like no other people in the history of the world.

**Follow Your Dreams: circumstances and obstacles are only
opportunities along the way.**

In chapter 6 we discussed why people do not follow their dreams. Perhaps this would be a good place to list all the reasons why people **do** follow their dreams.

1. Money: When you do something you love, quite often you become very good at what you are doing. The better you are at your trade, the more money you will make. Sam Walton proved this.

2. Health: Quite often following your dreams is better than living under the rules of other people. Janice Guthrie proved this.

3. Happiness: Following your dreams allows you to get in touch with why you were placed here on earth. Following that purpose is the quickest way to happiness. David Marsh proved this.

4. You can make a difference: To illustrate this I must tell you about a hero of mine who has followed his dreams. His name is Warren Buffett. He started out as a humble worker and ended up buying and selling companies. He is the founder of Birshire Hathaway, a holding company with investments in Geico, Gillette and Coca Cola. Today his company's stock is the most pricey on Wall Street.

His investment advice is to buy companies you can understand, that service a large number of people and hold them until they cease to be good companies. "I love going to bed knowing millions of men around the world will wake up and reach for their Gillette razor to start the day and later that day, they, their wives and their children are likely to drink a coke."

The reason Warren Buffett is listed in this book is because of what he is building. If Mr. Buffett continues as he has over the past few years he will leave a charitable foundation of well over $100 billion. This foundation will be a legacy that will help millions of people for generations after Warren Buffet dies. Mr. Buffett is "planting trees under which he will never sit."

And this is one of my goals. I may not be able to leave $100 billion, but I could leave $3 million. I can plant a tree under which I will never sit and I intend to do just that. What is your dream? What will be your legacy?

These people who have followed their dreams have made a difference in millions of people's lives. Collectively they have started businesses that have employed millions of people and paid billions of dollars in taxes. Your name can be added to this list.

Follow Your Dreams: you too can make a difference in this world.

SECTION II

Turning your Dreams into Reality

"Great ideas are a dime a dozen. It is people who can put them into practice that are priceless."

unknown

Jack Parr, the famous comedian, once said, "To steal from one person is plagiarism. To steal from 1,000 people is called research." Well, I will admit that the information you are about to read is compiled from hundreds of different resources. I have been fascinated all my life by people who have started with nothing and decided to dream big. I have been even more impressed with those people who were able to turn those dreams into reality.

From the time I was in the seventh grade, I have read the biographies of the great industrialists like Andrew Carnegie and Henry Ford. I have read the biographies of great people like Martin Luther King, Jr. and Billy Graham. When I got older and in business, I began to read the material of Denis Waitley, Robert Schuller and Napoleon Hill. It has been fascinating to me to learn from the lives of these people. I like to identify with these people and use their lives as inspiration for me to overcome the obstacles in my life.

To me it was never enough to have a dream. I wanted to make that dream come true. In following my own dreams, I have compiled the best of my research into a series of 8 steps that anyone can use to take any dream from an idea to reality.

I know my steps work for you because I used these steps to move from my brokenness to where I am today. These steps can help you accomplish anything you want, from a great home life, to a trip around the world, to that special dream you have inside.

At the beginning of each step you will notice a quote. This quote is designed to serve as an anchor to help you remember the step. After the discussion of each step you will notice a section called "tools." These tools are designed to give you a way to implement that step in your life today.

What do you want to accomplish? Read this section and make notes about your dreams in the margin.

"Without a vision the people perish."

Jewish book of wisdom

Chapter 11

Step #1: Vision

The first step to turning your dreams into reality is to establish a vision. A vision is simply a picture of what you want to come true. The clearer the picture of your dream and the more details you can describe, the easier it is for your dream to come true. The problem is most people never take time to think about the complete details of their dreams.

What will your dream look like as you begin today? What will it look like in five years... in 10 years... and in 30 years? Can you draw a picture of that vision? Can you use words to paint the picture of where you want to be? Can you use graphs of the numbers to visualize the dream you want to come true? Take time to draw that vision as many ways as you can.

As far as I am concerned this step is the easiest step because it is the most fun. You can dream of things that make you feel good. You can dream of big things for your profession. You can dream of big things for your family and for your finances. If you have big dreams, this is the place for you to express them.

I love the story of Walt Disney. When he was building his famed Disneyland in California, Walt Disney devised a plan to get his vision into the minds of the construction workers. He instructed the contractors that the first thing to be built would be the Magic Kingdom castle in the middle of the park.

Under normal procedure a construction team would build road grades, drainage and then rough roads first. But this was no normal construction. Disney instructed the construction crews to build and complete the Magic Kingdom castle first. Then Walt

Disney threw a party. He invited all the contractors, subcontractors, bankers, architects and laborers, everyone who would be involved in building the park.

The party included food, music and plenty of time for the workers to walk through the castle, touch its walls, see its splendor and feel its magic. Then Disney had everyone sit down on the hillside. As the crowd grew silent, Walt Disney strolled to the loud speaker and unveiled the plans for the rest of the park. He had the gathering to look toward the front of the castle as he described the glamour of main street. He directed their attention to his right as he painted a picture with his words of theaters, shops, roller coasters and games. He gave them a vision of the future of Disneyland!

The story goes on to describe that with a clear vision, those workers were able to open that theme park on schedule. This was the first major project of its time to open up on schedule.

The Jewish book of wisdom says, "Without a vision people perish." But I want to say that the converse of that is also true, "With a vision people flourish!"

In a recent poll of American adults conducted by the Barna Research Group of Glendale, California, 95% of Americans placed a "clear purpose in life" as the number one thing they wanted and needed most. Developing a vision for your life is one way to bring about this clear purpose.

Psychologists have also found that each of us have a picture in our heads of what we know is true. And physically, emotionally, spiritually, mentally and socially we move toward the picture we have in our minds. If we want to make a change in our lives, including following a new dream, we need to change the picture we have in our minds. The way we change this picture is by giving our minds a **new** vision. This is why a vision is so powerful.

A great example that shows how powerful visions are is the story of Leonard Schaeffer who was president of Blue Cross of California in 1986. The non-profit health insurer was losing $165 million a year. Schaeffer began his term as president by asking his managers one question: 'what business is Blue Cross in?'

Schaeffer states, "I thought they would say health insurance. But they didn't. They in effect said, 'We're in the business of being Blue Cross.' Being Blue Cross is not a business. It's more of a hobby. No wonder the company was losing $165 million; they had no idea what they were doing. They could not even answer the question, 'what business are we in?'.

The company's floundering was directly related to not having a clear vision for their business. "Without a vision the people perish," and perishing is exactly what the company was doing.

The first thing Mr. Schaeffer did was to change the vision of the firm from 'being Blue Cross' to **"being the best health insurance company in California."** With this clear vision, Blue Cross workers had a goal to work toward. In 1993, the company had a cash position of $1 billion! Vision is powerful and forces us to change our lives.

The same is true for Ford Motor company. In the 70's, all the American auto companies were losing money. The quality of their automobile could not compare with the improvements the Japanese were making and the Japanese were beating their brains out in the market place. For example, in the 70's the typical American automobile was getting 18 miles per gallon while a similar Japanese automobile was getting 30 miles per gallon. Ford knew they could compete with the Japanese, but they could only do it if their product had the same quality as the Japanese products.

Ford implemented the mission statement, "Quality is Job #1." And it was a joke. Everyone from the consumer to the labor workers laughed at this promotion. You may remember the commercials because Ford even hired comedian Bill Cosby to deliver the mission statement in the commercials.

The workers saw the slogan and finally accepted the company's commitment to change. It took the entire decade of the 80's to change the Ford Motor company, but today the company is competing and competing very well. "Without a vision people perish." The converse of that is also true: "With a vision people flourish!"

Martin Luther King, Jr. understood the power of vision. In his sermons and speeches during the civil rights movement he constantly kept a vision of a better America in front of all of us. At his highest moment, it is interesting to note that Martin Luther King, Jr. did not stand in front of 250,000 people in Washington, D.C. and say, "I have a strategic plan." No! What did he say? He stood and said, **"I have a dream!"** Why? Because when you have a dream, you have something for which to live. You have a reason to get up in the morning and a specific plan to follow. That is why dreams are so valuable.

Research has found that if people do not have a vision for their life, they begin to die. The body does not have a reason to stay around. So it develops cancer or some other disease. The same research has also shown that people who have something to do can live a long time.

Although this research is documented in several places, one of its earliest places is in the book, **Man's Search for Meaning** by Dr. Victor Frankle. Dr. Frankle found that people in the concentration camps of World War II had to make a decision. Those who decided they had nothing to live for and that life was meaningless, died very soon. But for those who decided that life had meaning and that there was something to live for, even if the only reason was to get back at the guards, they survived.

Another example is coach Bear Bryant of the University of Alabama. Bear Bryant always had a game and a new season to which he could look forward. When he retired, however, the vision of his life was gone. He lived only 6 days after his retirement.

Some insurance companies have documented this vision so carefully that they give high-powered executives about 16 months to live in retirement. Many die within months of retirement, because they have no vision for their retirement years.

But the opposite is also true. Dr. Bernie Siegel, a medical doctor and author in New Haven, Connecticut, tells the story of John Florio in his new book, "Peace, Love and Healing." John was a landscape gardener who was diagnosed with stomach cancer. It was suggested to John that he have surgery immediately. John told his doctors, "You forgot something. It's springtime. I'm a landscape gardener, and I want to make the world beautiful. That way if I survive, it's a gift. If I don't, I will have left a beautiful world." He had a vision for what he wanted to do with his life and the world around him.

Four weeks later he had surgery. The pathology reports revealed that he still had a lot of cancer left in his body after the surgery. Seven of his lymph nodes were positive for cancer. His doctors advised chemotherapy and X-ray therapy. But the doctors had forgotten his vision. It was bigger than his cancer. He told them, "It's still spring. I don't have time for all that treatment." He was at peace and he healed rapidly.

Four years later he returned for a check-up. He needed a hernia repaired. His cancer was completely gone. John recently celebrated his 83rd birthday. As Dr. Siegel puts it, "You have to wonder - what has happened to his cancer?" Without a vision people perish. With a vision you can live!

Vision is a powerful force. It can pull some people through concentration camps. It can pull some people through cancer. And it can pull you through your obstacles to reach your dreams.

Set your visions; they are indicators of the future; they will give you something to live for, and will change your life. What would you do if you knew you could not fail?

As I have told you, I take this process very seriously. And as we go through this 8 step process I would like to give you a personal example from my own life. Remember, in 1984 I was bankrupt and living on borrowed money. I took a notebook and began to ask the question, "What would I do if I knew I could not fail?" In answering that question, I dreamed of plans for 100 acres of land. I wanted a place where animals could live, a place that could never be destroyed and that I could pass on to my children and grandchildren.

This became my vision. In an attempt to make this vision very clear, I drew the plans for the 100 acres with a 2,000 square foot house in one corner, with trails going through the wilderness, a lake just below the house and a grove of pecan trees surrounding the lake.

How clear is your vision? The clearer you can make your vision the better your chances to accomplish your dream.

Tools

There are two tools you may want to employ today to begin to paint a vision for your life.

Tool #1: Develop a Vision Book. From your local office supply store, obtain a blank notebook you can write in. I actually bought a book with clear plastic pages inside in which I could slide pages of drawings and text. In your book write out what you would do if you knew you could not fail. If appropriate, draw a picture of that vision. Complete a page of text and a picture of each of your dreams.

Tool #2: Write a mission statement. As a speaker and author, I have many people come up to me after a presentation and say, "I have dreams all over the place. I have dreams for my house, family, career, my body, etc. How can I coordinate these? They seem to be too much to handle." This is a good question. The answer is to develop a mission statement for your life. A mission statement is a one sentence statement that describes what you want to do with your life. If you can put the essence of all your goals and values into one statement what would it be? You can then place all your dreams in relationship with that mission.

By way of example let me give you my mission statement: "To create a positive difference in the world in which I live." Every dream and goal I have is designed to fulfill this mission. In other words the dreams I have for my business are dreams of profitability, efficiency, growth, etc., but the purpose and end of all my business activity is to 'create a positive difference in the world in which I live.' The same is true of my financial goals, my dreams for my family, etc. A mission statement can give you a general purpose for all your activity. Each individual goal can give you a way to fulfill that mission.

South Central Bell has a great mission statement. It reads "to bring people together through communication." Every department in the South Central Bell organization took this as the beginning and wrote their own mission statement. For example the marketing department's mission statement is "Bringing people together through communication by marketing efficiently the products of South Central Bell."

What is your mission statement? Write it out.

"Most dreams of glory are safe, because we never venture to put them into practice."

Charles Curothe

Chapter 12
Step #2: Bet Your Life

Some of the most sobering words I have ever heard came at my grandfather's funeral. The minister rose to the pulpit and stated, "A. C. Stone lived 76 years, 2 days and **17 minutes.**" It hit me like a ton of bricks. **We do not have years to live; we have minutes to live.** And we only have a limited number of these minutes to live.

If you and I only have a limited number of minutes to live on this earth, we had better start living them for something worthwhile — like our dreams. I decided to start taking advantage of every moment of my life.

A recent national survey stated that 48% of Americans[5] had no belief in their life that they would die for. And yet many of these people will go to work 8 and 10 hours a day, day after day, 50 weeks a year literally exchanging their lives for their paycheck. Yes, in essence we are exchanging our lives for our jobs. And that is OK. But if we are going to exchange our lives for something, it might as well be something we want to do. It might as well be something of value that can make a difference in this world; **it might as well be our dreams.**

So the question comes, "Is your dream worth exchanging your life for?" If you are going to exchange your time and energy for the fulfillment of your dream, then betting your life is exactly what you are doing. If your dream is not worth exchanging your life for, don't follow that dream. Find another dream because for any dream you expect to come true, you are going to have to exchange your life for it.

[5] "The Day America Told The Truth" by James Patterson and Peter Kim. Prentice Hall Press 15 Columbus Circle, New York, NY 10023. A comprehensive survey of the American Nation.

After giving one of the finest concerts of his life, a great pianist was approached by a lady who was overjoyed by his performance. "Oh, I would just give anything to be able to play the piano like that." The pianist answered "No, you wouldn't. You see I did give everything to be able to play the piano like this. When the other kids played baseball after school, I did not. From the time I was six, I played the piano everyday after school. When the other students dated and went to parties in college, I was in my room studying the piano. Today, people I know have joined literally thousands of clubs and social organizations. They have great lives and families and I am confined to practicing, memorizing and traveling. You see, I have given my life to be able to play the piano like this. I don't believe you would be willing to give anything." Just like the pianist has given his life to be able to play the piano, we have to be willing to exchange our lives for our dreams.

For years people have tried to interest me in playing golf. My answer is and always will be "no." I do not want to exchange the time and energy of my life for the ability to play golf. I am willing to exchange my life to help a friend who is in trouble. I am willing to exchange my life to learn to hang glide and play softball, but not to play golf.

My dream of having 100 acres of land was worth exchanging my life for. From the time I first had the idea until I got the deed to the property took 8 years. I did not spend all of my life on that project, but I did spend part of those 8 years on the project. When I finally got serious about buying the property it took me about three years of shopping to find the perfect piece of land. It took another 6 months to sell myself and my family on the idea and it took several months to get educated on the legal process to acquire the land. I did exchange 3 years of my life for this property, and it was worth it.

In October of 1992, my wife and I bought 110 acres of Kentucky woodlands. The property sits on a 45-acre lake. We now own 15 acres of the 45-acre lake, plus 10 acres of cleared land and 85 acres of woods. There are bass, crappie and catfish in the lake. The woods are home to squirrels, rabbits, deer, coyotes, turkey and possibly bobcats. It is one hour from my home and we bought the property for $299 an acre. Your dreams can come true, too, if you are willing to bet your life on them.

I love to tell the story of Dr. Martin Luther King, Jr. He could have been a great biblical professor, or a pastor of a church all of his life. He could have been a great politician. But he was willing to leave the pulpit and the class room to walk and live with his people. He was willing to bet his life on his dream of racial equality.

During the bus strikes in Montgomery, Alabama, there were threats on Dr. King's life. After an explosion at his home, Dr. King's supporters wanted to place security guards around his home and family. His answer was a firm and defiant "no." If he was going to preach non-violence, he was going to live non-violence. Dr. King was willing to bet his life on his dream. The reason people, like me, still speak of Martin Luther King, Jr. is because he did give his life for his dream.

Dr. King's exchanging his life for his dream is a dramatic example; we may not have to die for our dreams, but we do have to be willing to exchange the time and energy of our lives for our dreams. If your dream is not worth exchanging the time and energy of your life for, don't follow that dream! It is not worth it and you will probably not achieve it.

Tools

The tool for implementing this step is to take a vow. To literally say, "I am willing to exchange my life for this dream." If you are a sales person and you want to make $150,000 this year, how much of your life are you willing to exchange for that money? The salesman's vow might read: I, Johnny B. Good, do solemnly vow to exchange 40 hours a week, 50 weeks a year to earn $150,000 in the real estate sales for myself and family.

Now it's your turn. "I, _____ _____, do solemnly vow to exchange _____ of my life for the fulfillment of_____."

"Wherever anything is being accomplished it is being done by a mono-maniac with a mission."

Peter Drucker

Chapter 13
Step #3: Focus

How many horses can you ride at once? Unless you belong to the Chinese circus, the answer is one. It is impossible for the average person to ride 12 horses at once. And what happens if by chance you are crazy enough to try to ride 12 horses at once? You will be thrown off and trampled to death.

The same is true with your dreams. It is impossible to follow 12 dreams at once. You will not be able to do any of them well. In fact you stand a good chance of not being able to do anything at all.

I have trouble with this step because I want to do everything at once. It is very hard for me to focus my time and energy on one dream at a time. But I can tell you from personal experience I am far more successful when I focus my efforts on one dream.

While flipping through a magazine recently I saw the following sign,

"FOCUS OR DIE." I believe this is especially true today. People who can focus on one goal or dream or one business can be far more successful than those who try to do many things at once.

We can see this throughout history. Very famous people have been so focused, you might say they were bent. That is they focused so heavily on one dream or goal, their entire lives were devoted to their dreams. Their names in some cases become synonymous with their dreams.

Play a little word association with me. When I mention this person's name, write down the first word that comes to your mind.

Col Sanders.................................
Sam Walton ....
Henry Ford.................................
Thomas Edison...........................

These men have done a lot of things. They raised families, etc. But they have devoted their professional lives to the pursuit of just one dream.

Col Sanders.....................chicken
Sam Walton ....Wal-Mart
Henry Ford............................cars
Thomas Edison.............light bulb

The same is true for you. You may want to do a lot of things. But if you are serious about pursuing your dream, you must focus your efforts on one dream.

Many people will try to pull you away from your focus. They will tell you about this club and this association and how you can't live without this seminar. Although they have the best of intentions, they pull you away from your focus, and anything that pulls you away from your focus is **death to your dream.**

A 4,000 year old African story from the Housa country of Nigeria illustrates this point very well. A young boy was hunting ground squirrels with his father. During the hunt the young boy made a bad mistake. The more the father thought about the mistake, the madder he got. He eventually started yelling at the young man, and finally he said, "You cannot be my son any longer. I will not put up with this type of behavior." And he took the boy to the local village and left him there as an orphan.

Three days later, the king of the local area was passing through the village and he noticed the young boy living as an orphan in the streets. The King having lost his own son just a few months before, decided to adopt the boy. For the next 20 years the boy lived in the king's palace as the king's son and prince of the land. He ate the finest food, received the best education and was the envy of all.

Twenty years later, the young boy, now a fine young man, was riding his horse and noticed a bent over old man. As their eyes met, the boy knew this was his biological father. As they embraced, his father through the tears said, "I made a mistake. I should never have left you. Would you consider coming back and living with me and being my son again, and helping me in my old age?"

The young boy was confused. "What do I do?" He loved the King as his father and he had a great life. But he had always yearned to be reunited with his biological father, and to be a part of his life.

The king said to the young man, "Don't make a decision right now. Wait until tomorrow and meet your father and me out at the big Oak tree at the end of the village at noon."

The next day the boy was dutifully at the appointed place. Both his biological father and his king father came riding up on horses. They dismounted. The king drew a shiny new sword from the saddle of his horse and handed it to the young man. He said to him, "You cannot live in this world with two fathers. Today you must kill one of us."

You see the word 'decided' comes from the Latin, and it literally means to 'murder your options.' You must kill off all the other options you have and focus on one dream.

When I decided to be a professional speaker. I had to kill forever the option to become an accountant or truck driver. Those are no longer options for my life. If you decided to follow your dream, you will have to let the other opportunities of your life die.

To what have you decided... Murder your options.

Tools

The tool for murdering your options is to learn to say "no." It is hard to say "no" when you know you could do something. It is hard to say "no" when you know there is work to do and that people may suffer if you do not do the work. **But to be successful in your work and in following your dreams, it is essential that you learn to say "no" to those things that deter you from accomplishing your dream.** To say "no" is not to pass on doing something for right now. To say "no" is to literally murder the option.

My pastor, Phil Christopher, is fond of saying, "It is easy to say 'no' when you know what you have said 'yes' to." When you have said "yes" to your dreams it will be easier to say "no" to all the good opportunities that will distract you from your focus.

You have the right to say "NO!"

Do you have trouble saying "NO?"

____ A. your mother?   (when she asks for a ride or for you to do something) _____

____ B. your sister?   (does she have more needs than you have resources) _____

____ C. your spouse?   (when he wants to buy a "dream car" that is too much money) _____

____ D. your boss?   (asking you to stay late) _____

____ E. your friend?   (who wants to smoke or use drugs in your presence) _____

____ F. salesmen?   (Girl scouts, fund raisers, insurance, religious enthusiast) _____

____ G. a neighbor   (who wants you to watch 4 kids "for just an hour") _____

____ H. _____

Rules to saying "NO!"

1. Say "no" quickly.
2. Don't soften the "no" by agreeing to do something later.
3. Be honest.
4. Use phrases like, "If I do this, I would not be able to..."
5. Use phrases like, "I'm sorry, I can't."

"Dream in a pragmatic way."

Aldous Huxley

Chapter 14

Step #4: Write it Down

If you want to start a business and you go to the banker to apply for a loan, what would be the first thing s/he would ask for? That's right, a written business plan.

I have spoken to many bankers, who have told me that they do not care what is in that business plan. They know as soon as you open your doors your business is going to be different than you had planned. Life takes unexplained turns, customers want different things and your target market may change. Bankers insist on the business plan because they want **you** to go through the process of thinking about your business. They want you to think about it clearly enough to write it down. Have you thought about who your customer is? Can you write down a detailed description of them? How will your customers find out about you? Why is your product different from others on the market? The bankers know, if you have taken your dream from vague thoughts to the specifics of a business plan, your chances of succeeding are greatly increased.

If "writing it down" is good enough for bankers and entrepreneurs, it is good enough for our dreams.

When you write something down, it takes on a life of its own. Suddenly, it becomes clear in your mind exactly what you want. Your dreams become clear to other people, because they can read what you plan to accomplish.

My church is a great example of what I am talking about. For years our church was doing OK, but really floundering without a purpose or direction. We were doing some good things, but we were not really going anyplace. Basically we were just drifting.

I brought my concern about this to the attention of our pastor. I shared with him some of the things I have shared with you. I don't know if our conversation resulted in the changes or not, but soon thereafter, our church developed, and wrote, a mission statement. With the mission statement in place, we then developed and published a strategic plan for living out that mission statement. In following that plan, our church has developed a focus and something to do. Everyone from the visitors, to the membership, to our national convention know and understand exactly what we are trying to do. Today our church is in as good a shape as it has been in 20 years.

Two Studies

Two recent studies conducted by Massachusetts Mutual and AT&T concluded that businesses who have a written business plan succeed. According to both studies, only 40% of businesses have a written business plan that they follow. And those businesses are the ones that succeed. (David Gumpter Communications as reported on 1/19/94 on the Louis Rukiser show).

My Dream

In following my own dreams, I took one full year and I wrote down exactly what I would do if I knew I could not fail. I wrote in detail exactly what I wanted my personality to look like. What would my house look like? What would my 100 acres look like? What would my family look like? It was not easy; it was one of the hardest things I have ever done in my life, because I had to think out exactly what it was I wanted. I was careful not to put down lofty and vague goals, like "I want a house" or "I want a million dollars." No! I put down "I want 100 acres of woods, on the outskirts of Denver, 20 minutes away from the university where I could teach." I drew out detailed floor plans. I even planned rooms that I could rent to college students. I was very specific about the dreams.

Have you heard the old adage, "Be careful of what you wish for, because you just may get it?" This is very true. My dream of owning a home on 100 acres of woods with a lake and a pecan grove just 20 minutes from the University of Denver did not come true. As my life turned out I live in Louisville, Kentucky.

But I do own 100 acres of land on a lake and there are pecan trees on the property. My dream did not come true exactly as I had planned but it is remarkable how close to my written plan my dream did come.

So the question comes, do you have the courage to write down your dreams and make them come true? As proven by two studies, one of the crucial steps is to have a written business plan. This is the step that separates the men from the boys. This is the step that separates those who want to talk about their dreams from those who want to make their dreams reality.

Tools

Tool: In your dream book write a mission statement for your life and then write first, second and third steps for implementing this mission statement. Be as specific as you can as you write the details of your dream; be as specific as you can regarding your process for achieving your plans and watch your dreams take on a life of their own. Don't be discouraged if this takes a lot longer than you expect. Write down the dreams. They can and do come true.

"People spend more time planning a two week vacation than they do planning their lives."

Unknown

Chapter 15
Step #5: Strategy

If you are standing in your kitchen, and you want to go to the basement, you would need to know the one, two, three steps it would take to get to the basement. Now these steps may be so easy that you know them without thinking, but there are several steps to take, nevertheless. Let's detail them for a moment. First, you have to be willing to take the steps. Second, you have to know the general direction of the basement. Third, you have to place one foot in front of the other and start walking in the direction of the basement. Fourth, if you run into obstacles, shoes, walls, people, etc., you have to be willing to go around those obstacles to get to the basement.

Although this may be a simple example, it illustrates the type of plan one needs in following their dreams. No matter what you dream, it is essential that you write down the 1, 2, 3 steps. The first step is to get a pen and a piece of paper. The second step is to write down your goal. The third step is to eliminate all the things taking your time and preventing you from following your dream. You may not know all the steps toward the completion of your goals. That is OK. Write down the steps you do know.

Although there are several aspects to a strategic plan, generally a plan will include the following:

1. Business. What business are you in? This may be different from the product that you sell. There is a very famous story of the president of Rolex. When asked how the watch business was, he responded, "I don't know. I'm not in the watch business; I'm in the luxury business."

As the industrial revolution emerged in this country, many of our railroads concluded they were in the railroad business and stayed in that business. If they had concluded that they were in the transportation business instead of just the railroad business, maybe they would have survived as large transportation conglomerates, instead of losing business as they have as rail businesses.

What business are you in? Write it down as a part of your strategic plan.

2. Product. What is the product you sell? It is obvious that the airlines are in the transportation business. But the product they sell is plane tickets. The ultimate end to everything they do in business is to sell more tickets.

3. Target Audience. In business today it is essential to understand your target audience. Here are some questions to help you define your audience:

Who will buy your product?

What is the profile of the perfect client?

How do they like to buy?

Where do they live?

How often do they buy?

What type of marketing do they respond to?

4. Money. Every business will have to answer the question of money. How will you finance your operation? Where will the money come for planning and start-up costs? Please, be aware of this: most businesses do not fail because they have a bad idea, lack of customers or lack of start-up money. They fail because they do not have enough money to stay in business through the tough times. They lack staying power.

There is an old Chinese saying which illustrates this point. "It is much easier to open a store, than to keep one open".

5. People. Whatever your great enterprise, you will not accomplish it without other people. Who is going to help you with your business? You will need suppliers, bankers, accountants, printers, etc. Think through who will be helping you.

6. Computer. The future belongs to those who know how to use computers. It is not enough to know how to turn one on and to type a letter. Using your computer to do your accounting and taxes, your inventory and payroll, your client list and newsletters and having access and knowledge to the on-line services and libraries is essential.

7. Distribution. How will you deliver your product to your customers on time?

8. Operations. Who will do the following: billing, collecting money, depositing money, etc.?

9. Time. When do you plan to finish? Is there an end to your work?

10. Spanish. Ten years ago most people did not own a computer. Today everyone I know owns a computer. In the next 10 to 15 years the same will be true of Spanish. The Spanish population is one of the fastest growing populations in the world and in the United States, and most of us will learn to speak and deal in Spanish just like we currently have learned and dealt with computers.

11. Constant Learning. There was a time when we talked in terms of getting an education. No more. Knowledge is changing so fast, that today workers must prepare for continual learning. In the plan for your dream, how will you get your initial training and how will you continually learn?

12 . Constant improvement. Competition between businesses makes products and services better for the customer. The problem is competition keeps things changing all the time. In order for us to compete we must constantly improve our performance, service and products to keep up with the competition.

Mary Lou Retten, the Olympic gymnast, tells the story of standards in the Olympic world of gymnastics. According to Mary Lou, every 4 years the standards for a gymnast change. What is considered exceptional this year, will be considered standard at the next Olympics. The standards are always improving. This is the clearest picture of American business that I have seen in a long time. What is considered exceptional service or an exceptional product today, will be considered the standard a year from now. Do you have a plan for this type of competition?

13. Government regulation.   Because of all the crazy people out there who take advantage of others, the government has to regulate business. Your strategic plan will have to include how and who is going to deal with government regulation.

A recent poll conducted by Arthur Andersen concluded that the biggest headache of mid-size companies was government regulation. This outranked health care and producing a profit. The survey went on to say that the CEO spends about 6 hours a week working with government regulations and that the average mid-size firm spends 36 hours a week on compliance. Your business or organization will have to have someone deal with government regulation. (Source: August 1994 Success Magazine)

Lee Iacocca and Zig Ziglar have been very successful in their business lives. I thought I would include here the strategic plans that have made them successful.

Zig Ziglar's strategic plan:

1. Write it down.
2. Set a date for its accomplishment.
3. Identify the obstacles you must overcome.
4. Identify the people and groups you will need to help you succeed.
5. Identify the skills and knowledge you will need.
6. Get a plan of action.
7. List the benefits you will receive.

You can find a fuller explanation of Zig's plan in any of his books or tapes, which can be found in your local book store.

In his autobiography, Lee Iacocca describes a management plan I have always found helpful. He has his managers sit down with each of the people who report to them once every 3 months. They ask 3 questions:

1. "How did you do in the last 90 days in accomplishing your goals for that period of time?"
2. "What are you going to do in the next 90 days?"
3. "How do you plan to do it?"

Iacocca says this insures that his supervisors talk to their subordinates at least 4 times a year. They also have a way to evaluate a person's performance. Additionally, they have a way for the employer to adjust the employee's actions and plans if they are not high enough or if they are too high. Perhaps these questions would help you in your personal or professional growth; they have helped me.

In my plan to buy 100 acres of land, I had a very clear picture of what I wanted.
1. Within one hour of Lousiville, Kentucky.
2. It had to be worth more than I paid for it.
3. It had to be mostly woods.
4. I wanted a lake if possible.

I then developed a strategic plan for accomplishing that dream.

1. Convince myself this was worth my life and money.
2. Convince my wife of the same thing.
3. Watch the papers and real estate offerings for possible sites.
4. Talk to realtors.
5. Talk to potential investors.
6. Go to trade shows where tree lovers would be gathered.
7. Make speeches and proposals to several nature groups.
8. Put together money for the investment.
9. Talk to my family who would eventually share that dream.

The actual dream took more steps than these. But these were the initial steps I wrote down. It is a funny thing about life; we never know all the steps we need to take when we first start our dreams. But we do know a few of them, and we will never learn the rest of the steps until we first take the steps we have been given.

You may not know all the steps you need to take to accomplish your dream. That's OK. Write down the steps you do know, and start accomplishing them. You will find that as you do those steps you will learn the next steps you should take. The old Chinese saying states this well, "A trip of a thousand miles begins with one step."

Tools

Tool: In your dream book following your dreams and your mission statement, write a strategic plan that will allow you to fulfill that mission statement. Write the plan as though you were going to present it to a banker. Follow the guidelines in this section and begin today!

Often this planning stage is where people fail. They can dream. But dreaming is the easy part. Dreamers often fail to plan. And remember the old adage, "If you fail to plan, you are planning to fail."

No one said it was easy. Oscar Wilde once said, "Enjoy the colors of life and forget the detail. The detail is always vulgar." Mr. Wilde has keen insight; many people want to celebrate and enjoy the good and great things in life, but few people want to talk about the details and work involved in actually planning and accomplishing their dream.

You will notice in my logo the word "Follow" is very predominate. It is not enough to dream. We must be about following those dreams.

Personal Performance Contract

A personal performance contract is an attempt to put your projects into written form. The purpose is to give a step by step action plan for each project. The contract should include:

1. The reason for doing the project.
2. The outcome expected in the project.
3. The description of the project.
4. The time expectation.
5. The cost involved.
6. The action needed to accomplish the project.

This contract can be used for family relationships, for business activities or for personal goals. I have enclosed a sample copy. Please keep in mind that you can modify this copy any way you wish.

Personal Performance Contract

Date: _____

Location: _____

Contract between: _____

Name of Project: _____

Description:_____

_____

Goal (what do you want to do): _____

_____

Purpose (why are you doing it) To: _____

_____

To be completed by: _____

Major areas of completion:

Goal 1: _____

     step:_____

     step:_____

     step:_____

     step:_____

Goal 2 : _____

     step:_____

     step:_____

     step:_____

     step:_____

Signature:_____

Signature:_____

FOLLOW YOUR DREAMS

Long
Term
Goal

_____
_____
_____
_____

4

_____
_____
_____
_____

3

_____
_____
_____
_____

2

Short
Term
Goals

_____
_____
_____
_____

1

_____
_____
_____
_____

One Step at A Time

"There has never been a winner who did not first expect to win!"

Ralph Waldo Emerson

Chapter 16

Step #6: Expect to Win

Have you ever heard someone say, "I'm on a diet?" And in their very next sentence they say, "I can never lose weight on a diet." Maybe you have said this yourself. Have you ever heard a sales manager tell a salesperson, "You can be the best. You can sell a million dollars worth of our product; by the way, no one from your background has ever sold a million dollars worth of our product." What do you think the mind does when it gets a double message like that? What do you do when someone gives you a double message? Just like you, the mind does not know which way to go.

Psychologists have found that feeding ourselves contradictory information is very debilitating. We cannot function or work with two conflicting ideas in our minds. When the mind is given conflicting material it does not know which way to go and it literally shuts down. It is just like coming to a "T" intersection in the road and you do not know which way to go; so, you sit there in the intersection for a while. In psychology this is called the cognitive dissonance theory. The same is true of our dreams. Dreaming big and then repeating talk of self-doubt will kill your dream.

During a recent basketball game, I watched as one of the star players was driving toward the basket to make a shot with two opposing players between him and the basket. The player driving to the basket knew he was going to get fouled, because there were two opposing players in front of him. So, he drove toward the basket expecting to be fouled. He did not even shoot the ball!

This hit me like a ton of bricks. This was a picture of myself at work. I attempt a lot of things, but all the time I expect to be fouled; expect to fail.

Is this happening to you? Are you doing something expecting to lose or expecting to run into an obstacle? Emerson once said that no one ever won who did not first expect to win. Expecting to win is a must for following your dreams.

Our self-talk, our actions and our dreams must be congruent. The only way to achieve this type of congruency is through concentrating our thinking.

But before we can discuss how to concentrate our thinking, we must learn the oldest piece of wisdom known to humankind.

The oldest Philosophy in the world!

If I were to ask you what the oldest piece of philosophy known to the human race is, what would you say? Take a guess.

Here are some suggestions people have given in my seminars.

1. "Do unto others as you would have them do unto you." That is a good piece of philosophy, but that was first stated 1999 years ago by Jesus. Prior to Jesus, the closest thing we had to this philosophy was called, the silver rule, which stated "Don't do unto others, what you don't want done to you."
2. "The ten commandments." Well, this may be the oldest philosophy, but it's not what I'm after.
3. "Don't get caught." I heard that.
4. "To thine own self be true." Maybe, but that is not what I am after.

The oldest piece of philosophy known to humankind is, **"We become what we think about."** If it is not the oldest, it is the most universal because every religion and philosophy throughout the ages has said this in one form or another. Let me show you a few references to this:

The Jewish book of wisdom states, "As a man thinks in his heart, so he is."

The same book also states, "Without a vision the people perish."

Jesus said, "If you can believe, all things are possible to him that believes."

Marcus Aaurelius, the great Roman Emperor... "A man's life is what his thoughts make of it."

Ralph Waldo Emerson said, "A man is what he thinks about all day long."

William James, the great American psychologist: "The greatest discovery of my generation is that human beings can alter their lives by altering their attitudes of mind. We need only act in cold blood as if the thing in question were real and it will become infallibly real by growing in such a connection with our life that it will become real. It will become so knit with habit and emotion that our interest in it will be those which characterize belief."

Norman Vincent Peale: "This is one of the greatest laws in the Universe. Fervently, do I wish I had discovered it as a very young man. It dawned upon me much later in life, and I found it to be one of the greatest, if not the greatest, discovery outside of my relationship with God. The great law briefly and simply stated says that if you think in negative terms you will get negative results. If you think in positive terms, you will achieve positive results. That is the simple fact which is at the basis of an astonishing law of prosperity and success. In three words, BELIEVE AND SUCCEED."

William Shakespeare put it this way, "Our doubts are traitors and make us lose the good we oft might win by fearing to attempt."

George Bernard Shaw is quoted "People are always blaming their circumstances for what they are. I don't believe in circumstances. The people who get on in this world are the people who get up and look for the circumstances they want, and if they can't find them, they make them."

Dr. Robert Schuller: "We move toward the picture we have in our head."

As you can tell, this theme of "becoming what you think about" is replete throughout history. If you were to check any of the great religions or philosophies they would say it differently. Each of them have disagreed on thousands of things, but they have agreed on this one idea, "You become what you think about."

So what do we do with this? Well, some of our greatest contemporary psychologists, people like Denis Waitley and Lou Tice, have put it this way. People are basically visual. We have pictures in our head of what we think is true about the world; and physically, emotionally, mentally, spiritually and by our actions we move toward these pictures. We live out what we believe in our minds.

If we want to change our lives we have to change the pictures we have in our heads. If we change the pictures in our heads, we will physically, emotionally, mentally, spiritually and by our actions move toward those new pictures.

For example if you have a picture in your mind that you are 30 pounds overweight, then you will develop a lifestyle that supports that picture. You will no doubt have a diet, job and exercise program (or lack thereof) that will support your picture of being 30 pounds overweight. To lose the weight, simply place a new picture of the weight you want to be in your mind. Then you will develop a diet, job and exercise program that will support your new picture.[6]

How to Change the pictures in your mind.

"How do I change the picture I have in my head?" Some people have their pictures changed for them. For instance, they have a terrible accident that changes their bodies and thus they are forced to change their pictures. But most of us have pictures we have developed by years of casual choices, and we need to initiate a process to change these pictures to move us toward our dreams.

[6] This can be proven scientifically as well. The reticular activating system allows us as people to become aware of things. It is a selection system. It allows us to not listen to the humdrum noise of the day and to hear a baby crying. When we speak and think about one or two thoughts, we are directing the reticular activating system to look for opportunities in those areas. Richard S. Lazardus, *Patterns of Adjustment*, McGraw Hill, 1976, page 100+

The process for changing the picture in our minds is to replace the picture with a new picture. We need to dream of where we would like to go or what we would like to be and place that picture in our minds. Once we have our dreams in picture form, we need to develop ways to get that picture into our minds.

Here are three ways to change the picture in our minds.

1. Self Talk: Most people think at about 600 words a minute. It is estimated that we have as many as 72,000 thoughts a day. By using this self-talk to describe a new vision and by continually talking about this new picture, we can change our lives.

2. Anchors: An anchor is simply anything that will remind you of your new picture. An anchor can be a T-shirt with a saying on it. It can be your goals listed and placed on your bathroom mirror or car dashboard. It can be a saying or a poster you have on your wall. It can be a secret handshake you have with a fraternity brother.

I have developed a lapel pin, that serves as an anchor. It says "Follow your Dreams." Every morning as I search for this pin and put it on, it reminds me that today I will continue following my dreams. Throughout the day as people ask me what is on my lapel, I show them my "Follow your Dreams" pin. We talk about the dreams I have and it reminds me again. It anchors my dreams into my mind.

What are the anchors you have in your life? Check out the sayings on your walls and on your desk. Do you have one of those posters on the wall that says, "It's hard to soar with the eagles when you work with a bunch of turkeys?" Now that poster may have been cute when you first read it, but what is it saying to the coworkers who come into your office? What is it now saying to you every time you are angry with a colleague?

My sister used to have an anchor statement over her stove that said, "Some days you step in it and some days you don't." Wow, what a mind set to anchor in to!

3. Affirmations: An affirmation is simply a statement of what you want to be true. As you read these statements you will be sending a congruent message to your mind and you can change the picture you have in your mind.

Your affirmations need to be written in three ways. First, the "I am" statement. This is a statement that begins with the word "I am," and places your affirmation in present tense. "I am ....."

Second, the "I see" statement. This statement gets your visual process involved. You can paint a picture of what you want to be. As the new picture is formed in your mind, you will move toward that picture.

Third, the "I feel" statement. The "I feel" statement gets your emotions into the process. As you become emotionally attached to this new picture in your head, you will move toward that picture. You become what you think about.

Let me show you the affirmation I wrote for my speaking business.

> "**I am** a positive and exciting speaker. I bring excitement, content and confidence to the audiences I address. **I see** people leaning forward, taking notes and applying the material I have to offer. **I feel** my best having offered people the chance to change."

Can you see the I am, I see and I feel statements? I have been reading this affirmation twice a day for 2 years, and it has really improved my confidence, excitement and the content of my presentations.

When I was looking for the 100 acres of land, I had to keep talking to my wife, my relatives and friends. Reminding them, anchoring them into the idea that this was good and we needed to do it. I finally found the perfect piece of land within an hour drive of my home. When I was walking the land once, I picked up a small rock from a creek that runs on the property. I carried it in my pocket for 1 1/2 years. This was an anchor for me. Every time, I put my hand in my pocket, it reminded me of that piece of property and the dream I had of buying a 100 acres of land.

My wife and I also wrote affirmation statements for this project. In my notebook I carried the following statements: "I own 100 acres of land in Caneyville, Ky. I see myself fishing in the 45-

acre lake and hiking through the fall leaves. I feel a sense of elation having preserved 100 acres for the next generation."

Tools

Tool: First, get a notebook and write your affirmations. Write three sentences as clearly and precisely as possible. Place them where you can read them everyday.

Second, place the anchor statements in the form of posters, lapel pins, and sayings in your office and at your desk. These will remind you and others what it is you believe and what you want to come true.

Third, surround yourself with positive people who are on their way to accomplishing their goals. There is an old adage that says, "You will rise to the level of the people who are around you".

Fourth, when you are doing something at work or in your personal life, ask yourself this question. "How would the person I would like to be, do what I am about to do?" This will paint the picture of what you want to become. It will also elevate your level of performance.

Change that picture! **"There never was a winner who did not first expect to win."**

Psychologists in scientific research have found the part of the brain that helps us with our affirmation process. Richard S. Lazarus, Professor of Psychology at the University of California in his book, *Patterns of Adjustment* (McGraw-Hill Book, 1976 pages 100+), discusses the reticular activiating system. This system is involved in regulating the information that reaches our brain. When we are in danger this system opens up the brain and allows information to the brain so the body can get ready to protect itself. When we identify something as important, this system allows that information to reach the brain.

That is why the affirmation process works so well. When we affirm our dreams over and over in our brains, our reticular activating system can help us find ways to accomplish our dreams.

"Nothing in this world can take the place of persistence. Talent will not. Nothing is more common than unsuccessful men with talent. Genius will not. The world is full of educated derelicts. Persistence and determination alone are omnipotent. The slogan 'press on' has solved and always will solve the problems of the human race."

Calvin Coolidge

Chapter 17

Step #7: Persistence

If I were to ask you what you think about when you hear the word persistence, what would you say? If you are like most people you will answer with a phrase like "keep on going" or "hanging in there." I believe that persistence is far more than just hanging on.

I have found that when I "just hang in there," I hang on to my problems as well as the good things that I am doing. Persistence is more than just "hanging on." It involves moving past the problems we have.

There are two aspects of persistence that go beyond 'just hanging on.' The first is just to go as far as you can with the light you have.

Imagine, if you will, an old man with a long white beard, in a long white robe with a tall staff, holding an old kerosene lamp. (You know the old kerosene lamps with a wire handle, glass globe and a little yellow flame in the bottom. Do you have the vision?) With his right hand on your left shoulder, you are walking through a dark woods on a crooked dirt path. He removes his hand from your shoulder and says, "You walk ahead."

"Wait. I can't see," you respond.

"Sure you can," he says reassuringly.

"Well, yes I can see a little but I can only see about three feet."

And he replies calmly, "That's OK. **Go as far as you can with the light you have.**"

Trusting him, you walk down the path the three feet. When you get to the end of the darkness and about to take your first step into the dark, the old man lifts the lamp up higher until suddenly you can see three more feet down the path. When you walk those three feet, the old man steps up a little and lifts the lamp higher.

It is a remarkable principle of the universe. As soon as you walk as far as you can with the light you have, you are given more light with which to walk. The same is true with our lives and dreams.

Now this sounds pretty esoteric, doesn't it? Let me put it in easier terms. When I worked for Prudential Insurance company as a financial planner, I recall one day sitting at my desk with three sales in front of me. I had a fellow who wanted to buy an auto insurance policy, a lady who wanted a homeowners policy, and a young man who wanted and needed a $10,000 life insurance policy.

My problem, as anyone in sales can tell you, was I needed more sales than this. If I made all 3 of those sales, I would have only made about $280. I needed to make $30,000 within the next 12 months. For two days, I studied, worried and danced around about this problem, saying "I need $30,000. I need $30,000. How on earth am I going to make $30,000?"

Then finally I decided, "Heck, I can't worry about this all my life. I'm going to go make those three sales. Even if I go bankrupt in the process, at least I have made those three sales."

And do you know what happened? The guy who wanted to buy auto insurance had a neighbor who wanted to buy some car insurance. The guy who wanted to buy the life insurance also wanted a quote on car insurance in three months. And while I was out working with the lady who needed homeowners insurance, another lady called my office and wanted a talk to me about another type of insurance.

It was amazing. When I went and completed the three sales I had been given, I was given three more sales to work. When I went as far as I could with the light I had, I was given more light with which to work.

The same is true with any dream or goal you have. When you complete the steps you have been given, you will be given the next steps in your process.

In my search for the 100 acres of land, I talked about buying the land for 7 years. People would politely nod their heads and say "Yeah, that's a good idea." But when I actually completed the steps I knew I could do (that is first, finding the actual acreage, second, calculating the total price, and third, taking pictures and drawing up plans for its use), then I had people who were seriously interested in the project. When I completed the steps I had been given, the other steps became clearer.

This is a lesson on persistence. More than just hanging on, **persistence involves doing what you have been given to do.** Then and only then will the next steps in the process become clear.

The second aspect of persistence can be found in this little story. Recently, I was remodeling my kitchen. Like many people, I started on the easy projects first. I painted the trim and hung a new set of lights. The easy stuff. Then I ran into a problem; I needed to replace the counter tops and floor coverings.

As I walked into the kitchen to think about the remodeling job, I was proud of the work I had done. Then I realized that I did not know how to redo the floors and counter tops. Then I got distracted and would go and do something else. But when I came back to the kitchen, I ran into the same problems, namely the floors and counter tops.

Even though I was working and persisting in the job, even though I was 'hanging in there,' I kept running into the same problem — floors and counter tops.

So, you know what I did? I did what any self-respecting American male would do. I went into the family room and started building bookshelves.

Now that is a funny and tragically true story. But it represents the way many of us persist. We 'just hang in there' with the problems and the good things we have done. What I learned about persistence is more than just 'hanging on.' **Persistence involves finding the road blocks that are stopping you and developing a strategy around them.**

What should I have done? What I needed was a feedback system that would tell me where my problems were. Then I needed to develop a strategy to go around those problems.

We all have problems or obstacles that we are going to face in following our dreams. Sometimes we have trouble seeing those problems and we need to develop feedback systems that will allow us to identify those problems quickly and easily.

A feedback system may be many things. It may be your own critical thinking. Those of us who have spouses or in-laws have built-in feedback systems. (I hope that sounds as funny to you as it does to me.) Another way to have a feedback system is to have a professional or a mentor or a family member look at the project and help you identify the problems you are facing.

Once you have the feedback system, which will help you identify your problems, then you want to develop a 1,2,3 strategy to overcome those problems.

Using my remodeling project as an example, after about the third time of coming back to that project, I realized I was always encountering the same problem – I didn't know how to replace the counter tops. Once I identified what my problems were, I simply went back to step 5 and developed a **strategy** for getting around the problems.

My strategy was first to start a savings account that would help me complete the project. Second, I started talking to people who knew how to fix counter tops and floors. The remodeling project became easier because I had a 1,2,3 step process to go around my problems.

I believe the same is true of your dreams. If you are facing difficulties in completing your dreams, look to see if you are running into the same problem. Can you develop a feedback system to help you identify your problems and then develop a strategy to get around those problems?

If you go as far as you can with the light you have, and if you develop a feedback system and a strategy for getting around your problems, you will go beyond just "hanging on." You will go beyond just persistence and into the area of perseverance.

You may be surprised that once you identify the problems and a strategy around those problems, this will help you with other problems you may be facing with the project; problems like apathy and procrastination.

Tools

The tools for persistence are these.

1. Develop a feedback system to help you find the problems you may be facing. This can be your own critical thinking stimulated by the question, "What is stopping me?" or a spouse, family member, professional or mentor who can give you an additional perspective.
2. Develop a 1,2,3 strategy to overcome the problems you face.
3. Complete the steps you know you need to complete. In other words, "Go as far as you can with the light you have."
4. Write affirmation statements for accomplishing those steps.

Do you remember the story of Thomas Edison? Mr. Edison attempted 9,000 ways to invent a new type of storage battery before he found the right combination. His associate W. S. Mallory used to laugh at him saying he failed 9,000 times. But Edison simply replied, "I have found 9,000 ways it won't work." [7] This is true persistence. He had a goal in mind. He developed a strategy to accomplish his goal and continued through his problems. More than just 'hanging on,' he persevered!

---

[7]"The Thomas A. Edison Album" by Lawrence A. Frost, page 122, 1969, Superior Publishing Co., Seattle, Wa.

"If God is your partner, make big plans."

Dr. Robert Schuller

Chapter 18

Step #8: Faith

We started this 8-step process with talk about having a vision. Well, the last step in accomplishing your dreams is similar to the first. It is to have faith. By faith I mean trusting yourself, trusting your dream and trusting the process of life that you will get there. Faith is believing in your end result before you get there.

When a merchant ship leaves the harbors of New York heading for Hong Kong, the captain cannot see the harbor of Hong Kong for a full 99.9 percent of his journey. The captain does believe, however, that the Hong Kong harbor is there, and if he does the things he is supposed to do, he will reach his destination. This is faith. Believing in something you cannot see. This definition comes from the Bible. Hebrews 11:1 "Now faith is the evidence of things hoped for; the assurance of things not seen."

In his book "7 Habits of Highly Effective People," Stephen Covey states that effective people begin a project or a dream with the end result in mind. In other words they know what they want before they begin. With the picture firmly in their mind, the person has a very specific goal to work toward. This is another way to describe faith.

When I was dreaming of the 100 acres of land, I started with a very clear picture in mind. I had faith that I, my family and God could accomplish my dream. My faith made the work, the questions, the time, and the money much easier.

The same is true with your dream. If you start with a picture of your dream, if you can see the end result, if you can believe in the fulfillment of your dream, you will increase dramatically the likelihood of that dream coming true. You too can have faith in your end result. Keep your eyes on the end result, and you will move toward it.

Tools

Tools: The first tool to use for believing in your end result is to ask and answer the question, "What will the dream or project look like when it is finished?" This will point you in the direction you want to go.

The second tool I have found helpful is to plan a golden day. What would the perfect work day or day off look like? Describe it in every detail. This will give you a standard to shoot for in your work.

Third, answer the question, "How would the person I would like to be do what I am about to do?" This question is exciting because it gives you a way to improve your actions in alignment with your goals and dreams.

Chapter 19
Does This Work?

Quite often I run into a cynic who asks, "Does this stuff really work?" All I can tell you is my story.

As you know, in 1984, I was broke, unemployed and living on borrowed money. The family I had cherished had dissolved and the lady I loved had left. I faced physical problems and depression. From that broken place, armed with only the question 'what would I do if I knew I could not fail' and the above 8-step process, I began to follow my dreams.

Within six years, I had lived a year in Tokyo, Japan, developed a successful career in security sales, developed a portfolio of real estate, including a 110-acre game preserve, married a beautiful young lady and started my own business. All of this was accomplished by the time I was 32 years of age. I can tell you this 8-step process works!

There are other dreams I have accomplished using this system as well. They include:

- Earning B.A. degree in Religion
- Obtaining B.A. degree in Psychology
- Learning to Hang Glide
- Living one year in Nigeria, Africa
- Living two weeks with a Russian family in Slancy, Russia
- Developing the logo and product lines for my business
- Writing this book
- Adding an additional 60 acres to my nature preserve
- Forming the Creative Difference - a non-profit organization

I can tell you with certainty, this process works, because it has worked in my life. I know it will work for you!

My dreams have not stopped. I currently, have committed to:

Selling 50,000 copies of this book.
Selling 100,000 "Follow your Dreams" lapel pins.
Adding an additional $250,000 to my real estate portfolio.
Writing a second book entitled, "Spiritual Lessons I Have Learned."

What are your dreams? Where would you like to go? This eight-step process can help you to follow and accomplish your dreams.

SECTION III

Priming the Pump!

"We grow by dreams.
All great men are dreamers. Some of us let
dreams die, but others nourish and protect them
and nurse them through the bad days to the
sunshine and light which always come."

Woodrow Wilson

Chapter 20

Let's Prime the Pump

Many people have come to me with the question, "Where do I start?" I have gathered a few ideas that I hope will stimulate your thinking toward dreams you might like to accomplish.

1. **"What do you like?"** An old college professor once told me, "Conway, don't be afraid of your 'likes.' They are a part of your personality and who you are." I have always found that to be very good advice. When I have gotten involved with projects I like and have been interested in, I have always done my best work.

So in following your dreams take a good look at what you like and what you are good at. Do you enjoy playing chess? Volunteer to lead the chess club at the local high school. Do you enjoy learning foreign languages and learning about other countries? Volunteer to teach English as a second language through a civic organization or church.

2. **Get back to basics.** Abraham Maslow, a developmental psychologist, established a hierarchy of needs. According to Maslow, there are basic needs people have, such as food, shelter and security. People will seek these needs first and before all other needs in their life.

So in following your dreams, especially if you are going to establish a business, it is a very good idea if you can keep to the basics of life, e.g., food, housing, security, etc.

3. "Go where they ain't." If everyone is coming up with ideas in one area, go to another area and you will find a lot of untapped places to work and dream. For example, today many people want to have service businesses in the suburbs. So as an entrepreneur, how can we "go where they ain't?"

Well, many savvy entrepreneurs are building manufacturing firms in the inner city. Since much of America is moving their factories and plants to the outskirts of the city, this leaves the inner city a waste land. In the inner city, entrepreneurs are finding a great many people who are unskilled and desperately looking for work. In many cases these entrepreneurs are finding tax breaks, cheap, subsidized financing and plenty of labor.

4. Help people get grounded. Many people these days live very sophisticated lives, dealing with computers and intellectual ideas. Many of our relationships are conducted in 3 minutes around the water fountain or in a hallway. So, using the idea of "going where they ain't," many entrepreneurs are looking for businesses that will get people **back in touch with the ground.** Nature hikes, camping and fishing companies are doing great these days.

5. High touch. Companies that can provide high personal contact, to get people **back in touch with other people,** are also doing well. Bingo, square dancing, wake-up calls, book stores, even hair salons and bars with regular customers are businesses that provide high personal contact and are doing very well.

6. Find a need and fill it. If there are needs in your life or the lives of others, there is a job or a business or dream you can begin.

Self-fulfillment is a need. People will always want to do something better. Health, communication, better relationships, better spiritual needs are self- fulfilling needs that people will pay to learn more about.

Chapter 21

What if I am still not sure?

You might be saying, "OK, Conway, I have read this book and I still don't know what to do. I don't have a burning desire to do anything. What should I do now?" Well, there are two answers to that question.

First, start moving. If a boat is sitting still on the shore there is no way to get wind to its sail. But if the boat is put into the water, and it begins to move down stream, it can then collect some wind in its sails and be directed in any direction, even back up stream.

The same is true with you and me. If you are sitting on the sidelines, complaining, using excuses, and not moving, then life cannot steer you in any direction. But if you start moving, you can then begin to correct your course to do what you are supposed to be doing. So, if you are still searching for a dream worthy of committing your life to, start moving - join a health club, join a civic club, take a college course or volunteer at a local charity. This activity will hopefully inspire you to follow your own dream.

Second, buy someone else's dream. If you are still having trouble coming up with a dream of your own, why not join your time and energy with the dreams of other people who are trying to make a difference in this world?

The Boy Scouts and Girl Scouts are helping youngsters become adults. Big Brothers and Big Sisters are doing a great deal to help young children. I have enclosed in the back of this book, the names and addresses for Habitat for Humanity, the Nature Conservancy, World Hunger Relief and the Creative Difference. These are people who have dreams and are making a difference. Join their dreams and you may find the answers you are looking for.

Chapter 22

Living Beyond the Dream

I hope I have inspired you to follow your dreams no matter what your age or circumstances. But I realize some people have come to an age in their lives where they are not going to follow lofty or long range dreams. So what do you do if you have lived beyond the dreams of your youth; if you have come to a stage in life where you do not wish to pursue dreams? I have a few ideas.

1. No matter what your age or circumstances, **dreams can still come true.** I hope the examples of the 56-year-old man going back to college and the 100 year old woman running a $5 million carpet company will inspire you to set new goals and follow the dreams you do have inside. They can still come true.

2. **"Plant trees under which you will never sit!"** There are plenty of organizations where you can place your time, energy and money that will live longer than you will. You can give money to a young lady who is needy and going to college. You can inspire young kids on a basketball team with stories and gifts. You can invest your life into the lives of other people who will live longer than you will live. Find someone else's dream and invest in it.

3. **Become a Wounded Healer.** Who is the best person to help someone who has gone through a divorce? That's right, a person who have themselves gone through a divorce. Who is the best

person to help someone who is going through bankruptcy? It is someone who has gone through bankruptcy. The same could be said for the loss of a child, the loss of a job, etc.

One of the things you can do with your remaining years is to use the experience you have to help other people who are going through the same situations. Embrace the fact that you have faced some severe problems and find some people who need help facing those same problems. This is a great way to become a wounded healer and to live the rest of your life.

4. Enjoy Life. If life is a gift, the best way to say thank you for a gift is to use it. Enjoy the remaining years of your life. Do the things you like to do.

If you have lived beyond the dreams of your youth, you can still follow some dreams and accomplish some goals with the rest of your life.

Chapter 23

My Dream

I have asked you several times to write down your dream, to answer the question, "What would you do if you knew you could not fail." It might be appropriate for me to share with you some of my dreams for the future. I hope this will in some way stimulate your thinking regarding dreams you wish to accomplish.

The purpose of my life and the mission statement I have written for myself is, "To create a positive difference in the world in which I live." It is my dream to accomplish this mission in every aspect of my life.

Family: My wife Polly and I have adopted this mission statement for our family and our home. Our work together, in our church and with our personal friends is designed to create a positive difference in this world. By way of example, Polly teaches the 3-year-old children in our church. This is a way for her to make a difference with the children of our church.

My Business: The purpose of my speaking business is to inspire people to 'make a difference in this world by following their God given dreams.' I fulfill this mission with keynote addresses, seminars and retreats for companies, association meetings and conventions. I also fulfill this mission by volunteering for the "I Have a Dream" Foundation. My goal is to influence 100,000 people per year.

Products: In addition to my motivational presentations, I have created the "Follow your Dreams" collection. This collection includes books, tapes, T- shirts, and lapel pins to inspire people to action.

Dream Weekend: Twice a year, I have the pleasure to offer "Follow Your Dreams" retreat weekends. This weekend will take people through the process of writing a mission statement, brain storming about their dreams, writing strategies and affirmations to accomplish those dreams.

Dream Cruise: Our company is looking forward to sponsoring a "Follow Your Dream" cruise. This cruise is designed primarily for fun and relaxation; however, seminars will be conducted on "Following your Dreams."

The Creative Difference Foundation: In 1993, my wife, Polly, and I established The Creative Difference Foundation. This foundation is set up to create a positive difference in this world. We do this by establishing endowments. Once a year, we take 90% of the interest produced by these endowments and give it to organizations like Habitat for Humanity and the Nature Conservancy. (The other 10% stays in the endowment to help it grow.)

There are several advantages to this foundation:

First, since we donate money to a specific organization for a specific purpose, we can guarantee that 100% of the money that is given to us will go for food, tuition and building materials and not administration.

When people make a general donation to a non-profit's general funds, their donations are used for administration, distribution, insurance, cars, parties, advertising and hundreds of other purposes. Our organization can designate our money for a specific purpose. This can guarantee your money will be used efficiently.

Second, if a donation is given to a non-profit organization, that organization, usually spends that money that year. I was once at a church who took a $10,000 donation. They immediately went out and bought a $2,700 copier. By the end of that year all of the $10,000 was gone. A major donation, that someone spent their life building, was gone in 7 months.

Our organization can keep money like that in an endowment from now until the end of the earth. We can use the interest off the money for hundreds of years. Your gift will keep on giving.

Third, if an organization we give money to stops being a good organization, we can simply start giving to an organization that does good work.

This is an assurance that many donors do not have. If you gave a major donation to a very famous non-profit organization 20 years ago, you were helping poor inner city children. It was a good charity. But today that same charity has become a suburban health club. Our organization can assure people that their money will be channelled to good organizations that help people.

Fourth, in the future, this foundation will seek to help establish businesses, operated by entrepreneurs who are dedicated to making a difference in the world. These businesses will employ people and provide services to a community. Ultimately, the profits from these businesses will be turned back to the endowments of the Creative Difference and then used to help people.

We are on our way. We have already established two endowments one for housing and one for nature preservation. A portion of this book is going to these endowments.

I believe this dream is possible in my lifetime. My wife and I dream of leaving 3 endowments of $1 million each by the time we die.

"The end of wisdom is to dream high enough to lose the dream in the seeking of it."

William Faulkner

Chapter 24
Dreams do come True

I hope the information in this book will give you the inspiration you need to follow your dreams and to provide you with the tools you need to accomplish those dreams. The reason this is so important is because we as Anonymous Americans are the ones who make this world what it is. We make things happen here. Your dreams, no matter what they are, can come true!

The news media likes to tell us how bad things are in this country. But the facts prove otherwise. Here are some facts reported in a recent copy of the Kiplinger newsletter.

1. The US is the world's biggest producer of goods and services. We produce 66% more than Japan and more than all of Europe combined.
2. For the past 4 decades, the US has produced about 20% of all the world's goods. This figure has not changed since the 1960's.
3. We are the world's leader in output per worker hour.
4. The US is the world's low-cost producer in many areas including high technology and heavy industries.
5. We are the world's leader in export sales.
6. 20% of the US economy is in manufacturing. This is the same percentage as in 1960 and 1975. Of course, today we manufacture computers, scanners and prescription drugs rather than shoes and clothing as in 1960.

7. The buying power of the US worker is near the top of anyplace in the world.

What does all of this mean? The US is still the greatest country in the world, and dreams can come true here. These are the facts.

Allow me to relate a final story that emotionally drove home to me the idea that we live in the greatest country the world has ever known and that our dreams can come true.

Recently, my wife and I took a vacation in Nashville, Tennessee. On the Friday after Labor Day we went to the Opryland Music Park. It was one of those perfect days with the sun shining brightly, a 78 degree temperature, and there was virtually no one in the park. It was like we had the entire park to ourselves. We rode every ride 5 times without even getting off the ride.

Toward the end of the day, we stepped into one of the open air pavilions where about two hundred people gathered to listen to the music. The musicians and concerts at Opryland were great, but this particular group frankly was just terrible. So, I started to watch the people. On the front row was a big guy in a blue shirt, who looked like he might have fought in World War II. He had a big walking stick in his hands. This was a stick that had been stripped of all of its bark and varnished. It was beautiful. It even had an indention in the middle of the stem where a vine had once grown.

On to the left there was a young man in a pair of blue jeans with coal black hair and a moustache. He had his two-year-old little girl with him, who had long curly blond hair, wearing a little pink dress and dancing around in the aisle.

About half way back in the middle of the audience was a young man who looked like a factory worker. With him was his wife and two little boys who looked about 11 and 12 years of age.

Over on the right was a college student with long black hair down his back, that reached to his waist. He was wearing a T-shirt and a pair of blue jeans cut out at the knees. The left side of his head was shaved, and there was a Z design shaved into the side of his head. His look was beyond crazy; he looked scary.

Then the band got to their last song and started singing the words we all know...

"If tomorrow everything were gone,
I'd worked for all my life.
And I had to start all over
with just my children and my wife.

I'd thank my lucky stars,
I was living here today.
'Cause the flag still stands for something
and they can't take that away.

And I'm proud to be an American where at least I know I'm free.
And I won't forget the men who died who gave that right to me and
I'll gladly stand up, next to you.."

And when they said the words "stand up," I looked down and the old geezer on the front row took one hand and put it firmly on the top of his cane and he took the second hand and grabbed the middle of the cane and he started to stand up. When he got standing up, I saw the young man grab his two-year-old daughter and put her on his shoulders and the two of them stood up.

I looked back and the young factory worker and his wife stood up and they grabbed their two sons and made them stand at attention. I looked over and even old "Z" head had jumped up on his bench.

"Cause there ain't no doubt I love this land, God Bless the USA.
From the lakes of Minnesota" and about 5 people stood up and started clapping. *"To the hills of Tennessee"* and about half of the place stood up (we were in Nashville after all). *"From deep down in Georgia, from New York to L.A., there is pride in every American's heart and I'm proud to hear them say."*

And I looked around and 200 people were standing on their feet in honor of their country. And then something happened I had never seen happen at a concert. The entire assembly started singing with the band...

> "I"m proud to be an American, where at least I know I'm free.
> And I won't forget the men who died who gave that right to me.
> And I'll gladly stand up..."

And I looked down and the old geezer was hoisting that cane in the air. I looked over and the little girl was bouncing on her daddy's shoulders and clapping her hands. I looked down and even old "Z" head had his right arm in the air doing this Arsenio Hall dog call with his right hand.

> "Cause there ain't' no doubt I love this land. God bless the USA."

And it brought tears to my eyes to see this swell of patriotism sweep this audience. It reminded me that this is a blessed place; that you and I live in the greatest country the world has ever known, and that Anonymous Americans like you and me can still make a difference in this world by following our dreams.

Here's to your dreams,

Conway

SECTION IV

Motivational Resources

Motivational Presentations, Seminars and Retreats

Quite often I receive questions about my business and programs. Because of these comments I have enclosed a description of my presentations along with some of the feedback comments I have received. If your company has sales rallies, banquets or conventions please give our office a call at 1-800-459-3273.

Keynote Addresses and Seminars

"Follow your Dreams" is a motivational program based on the material in this book. With tons of energy, humor and interaction, I bring enthusiasm and content to your program. Your participants will be inspired to follow their dreams by my personal story, and by examples of other Anonymous Americans who have started with nothing and succeeded by following their dreams.

Purpose: First, to inspire Anonymous Americans to follow their God given dreams. Second, to provide an 8-step process anyone can follow to take a dream and make it a reality.

Objectives:
1. Inspire people to think about their dreams. "What would you do if you knew you could not fail."
2. To inspire people to think about their values. "Dreams are not an idea out of your imagination. They are a reflection of what you value."
3. To provide an 8-step process for taking an idea and making it real.

Attitude: "We become what we think about"

Attitude: "We become what we think about" is a motivational program based on the oldest piece of philosophy known to humankind. Not only do we, but the people around us and ultimately our world become what we think about.

Purpose: To inspire your participants to change their lives by changing their minds. Based on the quote by the founder of psychology, William James, "People can change their lives by changing their minds."

Objectives:
1. To show how we, the people around us and ultimately the world become what we think about and can be changed by our attitudes.
2. Provide practical ways to change our attitudes and change our lives.

Managing Change for the 21st Century

Based on the research of Dr. Gerald Westerhoff of Duke University, this program looks at the 4-step process each person goes through to accept something new in their lives.

Goal: To discuss change in a clear and understandable way, so your participants will be able to manage the massive change they have in their lives.

Objectives:
1. To present and understand the 4-step process for accepting something new in our lives.
2. To discuss why we resist change.
3. To provide a 1,2,3 step process for creating new things in our lives.

Balance: A Way of Life

Designed for the work-a-holic, this program teaches very practical steps to bring balance back into life.

Goal: To provide participants very practical tools for bringing a balanced perspective to life.

Objectives:
1. To understand why we are in the work-a-holic mind frame.
2. To provide practical tools, such as saying no and learning to dream, for obtaining a proper perspective.
3. To bring balance to life by providing practical ways to enjoy hobbies, family, romance and the spiritual side of life.

Retreats

Follow Your Dreams

A weekend retreat for people who want to follow their dreams.

Goal: "To provide participants with the inspiration and the planning to follow their God given dreams."

Objectives:
1. To answer the question, "What would I do if I knew I could not fail?"
2. To write a personal mission statement.
3. To write goals that the participant wants to accomplish in their life.
4. To write ways to accomplish those goals.

Strategic Planning Retreat

A program for departments or businesses who are interested in developing a strategic plan for their companies.
Goal: To facilitate your staff in developing a mission statement and practical strategic plan for implementing that statement.

Objectives:
1. To develop a mission statement.
2. To get "buy in" from all participants on the mission statement.
3. To illicit ways to implement this mission statement.
4. To illicit goals the staff wants to accomplish in the next 12 months.
5. To determine who is going to be responsible to accomplish those goals.

Products for Motivation
1-888-899-5353

"Follow your Dreams" lapel pin: A metallic pin perfect for the jacket or shirt. Every morning as you put it on and every time someone asks you about your pin, you will be reinforcing your dreams in your mind and the minds of others. We call these psychological anchors. This pin is perfect for a gift or as an incentive for your people. $5.00 each.

"Follow your Dreams" T-shirts: This blended "T" comes in 2 colors, Raspberry and Purple. These quality blended "T"s are perfect incentives, gifts etc. $15.00 each.

"Follow your Dreams" audio tape of a live performance of the above material. You will learn why people do not follow their dreams, where dreams come from and an 8-step process for turning your dreams into reality. $9.95 each.

"Follow your Dreams" video tape: A 60-minute live performance of the above material. This product is perfect for your sales meeting or top sales person. $29.95 each.

"Follow your Dreams" book: The book you have in your hands can be purchased in bulk for your sales staff or employees. Many associations give these away as speaker gifts each month. $14.95 each.

"Steps along the Journey" audio tape: This two-tape series contains 8 motivational presentations. Each presentation represents a significant learning point in the life of Conway. You will be asked to examine your values, look at who you admire and learn a practical way to make decisions. $14.95 each.

"Follow your Dreams" note cards: These cards are foiled embossed with metallic red and blue "Follow Your Dreams" and are perfect as gifts or to inspire a friend or colleague with their work. $1.00 each.

"Follow your Dreams" motivational card: This 2"x3" card sits perfectly on the desk, file cabinet or bulletin board as a constant reminder to follow your dreams. The reverse side also serves as a motivation with the words of George Bernard Shaw which says, "Some people look at the world as it is and ask why? I dream of worlds that never were and ask why not?" $50.00 for 100.

Resources

The following is a list of some of the books and programs that inspired my thinking and writing in this book. If you need further information please call.

1. Rich Wilkins and Company
    1026 Cobblestone Circle
    Shepherdsville, Kentucky 40165
    502-955-7269
    Products and programs to empower positive people.

2. Lou Tice
   The Pacific Institute
   Waterfront Place 800
   1011 Western Ave.
   Seattle, Washington 98104
   206-628-4800
   Programs and products to improve personal performance.
   "Mastering your Potential" is their current tape series.

3. "The Psychology of Winning"
   by Dr. Denis Waitley
   Nightingale Conant
   7300 N. Lehigh Ave.
   Chicago, Illinois
   1-800-323-5552
   Book, "Empire of the Mind," can be found in any bookstore.

4. "Unlimited Wealth"
   Paul Zane Pilzer
   ZCI Publishing
   Dallas, Texas
   800-460-4623

5. "Move Ahead with Possibility Thinking"
   Book by Dr. Robert Schuller
   Doubleday & Co. 1967
   245 Park Ave,
   New York, N. Y. 10017

6. "Think and Grow Rich"
   Book by Napoleon Hill
   Napoleon Hill Foundation
   Box 437
   Charleston, South Carolina

Habitat for Humanity
121 Habitat St.
Americus, Georgia 31709-3498
For local information- phone book

The Nature Conservancy
1815 N. Lynn St.
Arlington, Va. 22209
703-841-5300

The Creative Difference
500 Briar Hill Road
Louisville, Ky. 40206
1-888-899-5353

World Hunger Inc.
P.O. Box 639
Elmont, Texas 76640
817-799-5611

Roadmaps

Here are some roadmaps to some dreams that may stimulate your thinking.

Do you want to start your own Business?

1. Develop a Vision. What will your business look like? What is its name? Give as much detail as you can.

2. Bet your life. Would the completion of this business be worth your time and energy? Most start-up businesses require 12 to 14 hours a day. Are you willing to pay that price?

3. Focus. Be realistic. Can you give 12 to 14 hours a day to the fulfillment of this dream when other good opportunities come along?

4. Write it down. Can you put your dream into writing? Write out as many details as possible.

5. Strategy. What are all the elements you need to accomplish this dream? What are the first few steps for this accomplishment?

6. Affirmations. Write the "I am" the "I see" and the "I feel" affirmations for every stage of the business.

7. Persist. There will be problems including family and self-doubt. To accomplish your dream, you must persist through these.

8. Faith. Believe in your end result. By following this process your dream can come true just as surely as the sun will rise in the east.

Here are the best home businesses to start. Some you can start for less than $1,000.

Apartment Finding
Building Care
Home Cleaning
Street Sales
Car Washing
Cake Baking
Animal Care
Special interest Newsletter
Seminar on Business Subjects
Rental Property
Loan Banker
Daycare
Temp Services
Data Base Consultant
Recycling
Non-alcoholic Nightclub
Grocery Shopper
Landscape
Real Estate Appraiser
Bed and Breakfast
Amway
Party Planner

Sources: "199 Great Home Businesses you can start for $1,000"
is a book by Tyler G. Hicks, $12.95, phone 916-786-0426;
and "101 Best Businesses to Start" by Sharon Kahn published by Doubleday. Both are available at your local book store.

Here are 10 of the top 100 franchises in the country as rated by Success Magazine.

GNC Franchising Inc.	Retail	800-766-7099
Choice Hotels Internt'l.	Lodging	301-593-5600
Blimple International Inc.	Fast Food	800-447-6258
Coldwell Banker	Real Estate	714-367-1800
Sonic Corp	Food	405-232-4334
Money Mailer	Bus Service	714-265-4100
Merry Maids	Cleaning	800-798-8000
Snap-on Inc.	Tools	414-656-5200
ExecuTrain Corp.	Training	404-667-7700
Rocky Mountain Chocolate Factory		303-259-0554

Here are some organizations that may be able to help.

National Association of Cottage Industry	312-472-8116
National Association of Self- Employed	800-232-6273
Trade Show Bureau (set up at a trade show)	303-860-7626
Better Business Bureaus	803-276-0100
Small Business Administration	800-827-5722
National Assoc/Small Business Investment Co.	703-683-1601
Venture Line	518-486-5438
Center for Entrepreneurship	703-568-3227
Am. Woman's Economic Development Corp.	800-222-2933
Mothers' Access to Careers at Home	703-764-2320
National Association of Female Executives	212-477-2200
National Minority Business Council	212-573-2385
National Speakers Association	602-968-2552

Here are some of the most popular software applications for home and small business.

WordPerfect	800-451-5151	Word processing
BizPlanBuilder	415-254-5600	Business plan
MySoftware Co	800-325-3508	Database
Quicken	800-666-2562	Bookkeeping

Do you have a dream of being debt free?

Many people have a dream of becoming debt free. This is a great dream. Here is a 5 step process for becoming debt free.

1. Control your spending. You cannot spend money you do not have. Therefore, if you want to become debt free, you must spend less money than you earn. This is difficult. But one way to start is to eliminate things you do not really need. How much money would you have to spend if you eliminated newspapers, magazines, cable TV, second cars and cut back on eating out?

2. Don't let other people tell you how to spend your money. In America, we have a lot of people telling us how to spend our money. Every charity, church and good program is asking for money, "Just give a dollar." These dollars add up. We have a lot of pressure from family and the mass marketing system which ask us to buy gifts and cards, for bosses, secretaries, grandparents, birthdays, etc. Did you know there is a major holiday and gift giving activity every month in our country? The message is very clear: if you have a job, you must spend money on all these special holidays. But if you are trying to become debt free, don't let other people tell you how to spend your money.

3. List all of your debts. Take a piece of paper and list all of your debts. Many people have no idea how much they owe and how many debts they have. By listing your debts, you eliminate all guess work. Rank these debts from the lowest to the most expensive.

4. Pay off your debts. Take every penny you receive above your basic living and all of the savings from step number one and apply them to your #1 debt. One by one pay off these debts. This will give you confidence and help you become debt free.

To earn additional money you may want to start a new service to earn money to pay off your debts. Start mowing lawns, running errands or washing cars.

5. Don't incur more debt. Be careful, this process will only work if you are not incurring more debt. Don't place more pur-chases on your credit card.

6. Escrow your money for future bills. Take a look those major bills that hit your family throughout the year. Car insur-ance, life insurance, medical bills, Christmas and vacations hit every family every year. Estimate how much these bills cost you every year and set up a fund to make those payments. Call it the "IDHW" fund. (That stands for "I don't have to worry.") Put money each month into this fund. When these bills come due, you will have the money to pay them. This will eliminate the pos-sibility of future debts.

Do you have a dream of being rich?

Many people dream of being rich. Perhaps this is your goal. Here are a few steps for you to take toward that goal.

1. Define what rich is. Any goal must first be defined. What is rich for you? Is it having a million dollars? Is it having your house paid off? Is it having a steady income? Is it having no bills? Is it having a passive income? Maybe being rich for you is having 30 hours of free time a week. What is rich for you?

2. Develop a strategy. You must have a method for getting to your goal. How will you reach your goal? Will you start your own business, buy a franchise, open a restaurant or work with Amway or Tupperware? Will you invest in real estate, life insurance or invest in the stock market? Be sure you set a date for your achievement.

3. Pay yourself first. Start with a nickel a day. Place it in a jar. Call this your "I am rich" fund. This practice will help you develop a habit of being rich. You can even say to yourself, "I am richer today than I was yesterday."

Keep increasing your contributions until you are able to put away 10% of your gross income into this fund. Take all of your extra money (the money you have above your basic living needs and that you earn from your overtime work, new business, etc.) and place it in your fund.

Keep adding to this until you have 3 to 6 months in savings. Once you have your 6 months of living expenses, invest the additional money into a vehicle that will help you get rich. Any financial investor can help you with choosing the right investment.

Do not spend this money. The only way to get rich is to keep your money.

4. You will be surprised. You will be surprised how quickly your "I am rich" fund can grow. A $200 investment earning 15% a year will be worth $1.4 million in 30 years. $300,000 worth of real estate earning 8% a year will be worth $1.2 million in 30 years.

5. Develop your strategy based on the 8 steps for turning dreams into reality found in section 2.

Do you have a dream of getting into shape?

EXERCISE RECORD

Dream: _____

Purpose: _____

Attainable Goals:

1._____

2._____

The next 30 days:

Exercise/Time	Exercise/Time	Exercise/Time
1._____	11. _____	21. _____
2._____	12. _____	22. _____
3._____	13. _____	23. _____
4._____	14. _____	24. _____
5._____	15. _____	25. _____
6._____	16. _____	26. _____
7._____	17. _____	27. _____
8._____	18. _____	28. _____
9._____	19. _____	29. _____
10._____	20. _____	30. _____

Do you have a dream of reducing stress?

Dr. Vernon Coleman offers the following 10 steps to reduce stress:

1. Learn how to relax. Take up a relaxing hobby not a productive hobby. Play with children, take a walk and learn to relax.

2. Write a list of things that cause you to be stressed. Knowing the problem helps. Try to eliminate what is causing the stress, or find some ways to ease the situation.

3. Reduce your activities. If you have a stressful job and have stressful hobbies, try to reduce your exposure. Play a game for fun, instead of trying always to win. Get off of so many committees.

4. Complain. If politicians want to build a nuclear reactor in your back yard, don't sit and be angry. Write a letter to the editor, start a petition and let your feelings be known. This will reduce stress.

5. Learn to deal with panic attacks. If you get butterflies or headaches, take a huge breath. Count to four as you breathe in. Take a walk. Try to reduce the stress.

6. Buy yourself a rocking chair. The movement and the activity can help reduce stress.

7. Get away. When the stress builds up, find a place to unwind. Give the children to the family and get out of town. Take a day off work and stay in bed all day. Relax.

8. Find a share group. Find a group who can understand your problems and share your stress with them. There are many support groups, counseling groups and even Sunday School classes who can help you.

9. If you are planning a big project or party, don't commit everything to memory - make a list. Get people to help you, find those areas that you can't do and find some information and help for those.

10. Minor frustrations produce a great deal of stress. Learn how to handle those minor household chores, car repairs and even minor illnesses yourself. You may wish to take a class. Having the confidence to handle minor problems will reduce the stress that comes with those inconveniences.

Do you have a dream of getting an Investor for a project?

W. Keith Schilt, director for the Program in Entrepreneurship at the University of South Florida in Tampa, Florida says that "Running a profitable business is a lot more involved than coming up with a great idea." And the first step for getting money for your project is to prepare a solid business plan from the perspective of the investor. The business plan should include:

1. A clearly focused target market with growth potential. Who is buying?

2. A significant benefit for the end user. What features would prompt a customer to buy?

3. A record of past success. This will create a level of comfort for the investor. It is far more convincing to say people have used this product than to say people probably will use this product.

4. Have an active sales agenda including pricing, distribution and advertising.

5. Have advisors and an outside board of directors. Surround yourself with a team who can handle financial and marketing demands.

6. Create a financial arrangement describing return and monetary expectations. The project must give the investor a significant return for the amount of risk they are taking on.

Do you have a dream of Promoting Yourself or Your Small Business?

1. Business Cards. Print 2,000 and have a race to see how fast you can get rid of the 2,000 cards. Do something different with your card. Some people have a picture, others have a cartoon, one guy in health had a mood indicator on his card, another guy had his cards printed in 4" x 5". The goal is to have a card that is unique and that people will want to keep.

2. Professional Groups. Attend and get involved in professional meetings with people who can use your services. Chamber of Commerce, Rotary Club, Kiwanis Club, Professional Business Women and Computer Geniuses are just a few of the clubs. These groups can always use volunteers to help with the membership committee. Talk to people about your business.

3. Write an article that demonstrates your expertise in your field. Send it to newspapers, magazines, etc. being sure to include your name, company name, phone number and picture.

4. Network with others in your field. Let them know you are available to handle overload.

5. Talk with vendors from whom you buy products or services. See if they can use your services. Use their bulletin boards.

6. Offer to become a free speaker on your area of expertise for non-profit and civic organizations.

7. Network with your friends and family. The average person knows 200 people. If you have a newsletter for these people you will be in constant contact. These people can help you promote.

8. If you use a truck or car in business, professionally paint your name, slogan and phone number on the vehicle. This will be constant advertising.

9. Get samples of your product or work into as many hands as possible. This is called the puppy dog close. As people like your product, they will buy.

10. Run a contest with a fantastic prize.

11. Look for mail order companies who can use your product.

12. Ask existing customers for names of people who can use your product.

SECTION V

Quotes

The following motivational quotes have inspired and motivated me for years. I have included 365; one for every day of the next year. You may want to copy one or two of them for your desk or office, or pass them along to a friend. These may also stimulate your thinking as you write speeches or articles.

Although care has been taken for accuracy, I recognize that wisdom is attributed and passed along by many people in many ways. These quotes are offered as a way of inspiration.

All men of action are dreamers.
JAMES G. HUNEKER

Truth is God's daughter.
SPANISH PROVERB

If you get close to people,
you will catch their dreams.
ANONYMOUS

Don't sell the cow for a milk truck.
AUTHOR UNKNOWN

Following his childhood dream of drawing comic strips, a young
man was advised by an editor in Kansas City to give up drawing.
He kept knocking on doors, only to be rejected. Finally, a church
hired him to draw publicity material. Working out of an old
garage, he befriended a mouse who ultimately became famous.
The man was Walt Disney, his dream was Disney World,
and his friend was Mickey Mouse.
WALT DISNEY

If I am not me, who will be?
HENRY DAVID THOREAU

The harder you work, the luckier you get. Hard work makes you
very lucky. Coasting is only downhill. Life is in the burning of
the candle. They conquer who believe they can.
VIRGIL

Whatever you seek in the form of rewards,
you must first earn in the form of service.
UNKNOWN

The greatest psychologists in the world say we only
use 5% of our brain. If you could force your brain to
work at only half its capacity, you could learn 40 languages,
memorize the encyclopedia from cover to cover,
and complete the required courses of 3 dozen colleges.
DR. DENIS WAITLEY

Treat everyone whom you come in contact with as
the most important person on earth.
A MINISTER'S SAYING

There is no thrill in easy sailing. There is no thrill when the sky is
clear and blue. There is no satisfaction so sweet to take when you
have reached a destination you had never planned to make.
UNKNOWN

There is nothing good or bad, but thinking makes it so.
SHAKESPEARE

The person who rows the boat doesn't have time to rock it.
UNKNOWN

The temple of our purest thoughts is silence.
MISS HALE

Try. There is no try. There is only do or not do.
YODA (STAR WARS MOVIE)

Money is a good servant, but it is a dangerous master.
BONHOURS

Above all, to thine own self be true and it must follow as day follows night, thou canst be false to any man.
SHAKESPEARE

This world is divided into people who do things and people who want the credit. Do your best to be in the first class.
DEAN MORROW

If I have 8 hours to chop a tree,
I spend 6 hours sharpening my axe.
ABRAHAM LINCOLN

When you have a dream you've got to grab it and never let go.
CAROL BURNETT

It is easier to open a store than to keep one open.
ANCIENT CHINESE PROVERB

Know then thyself...the proper study of mankind is man.
SHAKESPEARE

A boss says "Go". A leader says "Let's Go".
ANGELO M. D'AMICO

What we have learned, we learned by doing.
ARISTOTLE

Lack of money is the root of all evil.
GEORGE BERNARD SHAW

One person with belief is equal to a force
of 99 who only have interest.
JOHN STUART MILL

He who stops being better stops being good.
OLIVER CROMWELL

It's been my observation that people are about as happy
as they make up their minds to be.
ABRAHAM LINCOLN

Be not afraid of Greatness: Some are born great, some achieve
greatness and some have greatness thrust upon them.
SHAKESPEARE

You're sure to lose far more pursuing security than you will
ever lose pursuing opportunity.
LAWRENCE THOMPSON

The beginning of every great success is desire.
NAPOLEON HILL

A house divided against itself cannot stand.
JESUS

Nothing can stop an idea whose time has come.
VICTOR HUGO

I've always thought that the actions of men are the best
interpreters of their thoughts.
JOHN LOCKE

Don't let the seeds spoil your enjoyment of watermelon.
Just spit out the seeds.
AUTHOR UNKNOWN

Dreams have only one owner at a time.
That's why dreamers are lonely.
ERMA BOMBECK

The first and worst of all frauds is to cheat yourself.
All sin is easy after that.
BAILEY

Speak only if it is an improvement on silence.
AUTHOR UNKNOWN

It takes a lot of courage to show your dreams to someone else.
ERMA BOMBECK

A little philosophy inclineth a man to atheism. A depth of
philosophy bringeth a man's mind about to religion.
BACON

To accomplish great things, we must not only act
but also dream; not only dream but also believe.
ANATOLE FRANCE

The end of wisdom is to dream high enough to lose
the dream in the seeking of it.
WILLIAM FAULKNER

Water at 211 degrees makes hot coffee. Water at 212 degrees
becomes steam and can move a ship around the world.
Move out of the hot water of mediocrity and into the steam
of outstanding success.

ZIG ZIGLAR

A dream only reflects the dreamer's thoughts.

JONATHAN ELEAZAR

Give a man a fish and you feed him for a day.
Teach a man to fish and you feed him for a lifetime.

LAO TZU

The unexamined life is not worth living.

SOCRATES

Just don't give up trying to do what you really want to do.
Where there are dreams, love and inspiration; you can't go wrong.

ELLA FITZGERALD

It is difficult to say what is impossible, for the dream of yesterday
is the hope of today and the reality of tomorrow.

BOB GODDARD

Dreaming is an act of pure imagination, attesting in all
men a creative power, which if it were available in
waking would make every man a Dante or Shakespeare.

H. F. HEDGE

My life seems to be one long obstacle course
with me as the chief obstacle.

JACK PARR

When we can't dream any longer we die.

EMMA GOLDMAN

All men dream: but not equally. Those who dream by night in the
dusty recesses of their minds, wake in the day that it was vanity:
but the dreamers of the day are dangerous men, for they may act
on their dreams with open eyes, to make them possible.

T.E. LAWRENCE

I thank God I live in a country where dreams can
come true, where failure is sometimes the first step to success,
and where success is only another form of failure if
we forget where our priorities should be.

HARRY LLOYD

My dream is of a place and a time where America will once again
be seen as the last best hope of earth.

ABRAHAM LINCLON

**We make a living by what
we get. We make a
life by what we give.**

WINSTON CHURCHILL

No one should negotiate their dreams. Dreams must be free
to fly high. No government, no legislature, has a right to
limit your dreams. You should never agree to
surrender your dreams.

JESSE JACKSON

I don't design clothes, I design dreams.

RALPH LAUREN

Every person is an architect of his own fortune and future.

APPIUS CLAUDIUS

Nothing happens unless first we dream.

CARL SANDBURG

There are those who will say that the liberation of humanity, the
freedom of man and mind is nothing but a dream.
They are right. It is the American Dream.
ARCHIBALD MACLEISH

It is better for a city to be governed by a
good man than by good laws.
ARISTOTLE

If you want your dreams to come true, don't sleep.
YIDDISH PROVERB

Commit yourself to a dream. Nobody who tries to do
something great but fails is a total failure. Why? Because
he can always rest assured that he succeeded in life's most
important battle; he defeated his fear of trying.
DR. ROBERT SCHULLER

The definition of growing up or becoming mature is taking
responsibility for actions both good and bad.
ANONYMOUS

Of all the people who will never leave you, you're the only one.
JOE CHARPBANO

Motivation gets you started. It is your habits that get you there.
WILLIAM JAMES (ATTRIBUTED)

Nothing in this world can take the place of persistence. Talent
will not. Nothing is more common than unsuccessful men
with talent. Genius will not: the world is full of educated
derelicts. Persistence and determination alone are
omnipotent. The slogan "press on" has solved, and always
will solve, the problems of the human race.
CALVIN COOLIDGE

Man, know thyself. All wisdom centers on this.
CARL JUNG

Don't part with your dreams. When they are gone you may
still exist but you will have ceased to live.
MARK TWAIN

The word "decide" comes from Latin and it literally means
"to murder your options."
PAUL DUKE

Life is simply a matter of concentration. You are what
you set out to be. You are a component of the things
you say, the books you read, the thoughts you have, the company
you keep, and the things you desire to become.
AUTHOR UNKNOWN

All sunshine makes a desert.
AUTHOR UNKNOWN

The key to success is simple. Make people dream.
GERALD deNERVAL

What you want to do, and what you can do,
is limited only by what you can dream.
MIKE MELVILLE

Sow a thought and you reap an action. Sow an action and you
reap a habit. Sow a habit and you reap a character.
Sow a character and you reap a destiny.
AUTHOR UNKNOWN

Dream in a pragmatic way.
ALDOUS HUXLEY

Don't sweat the little things, and remember,
they're all little things.
SOMEONE TRYING TO BE FUNNY

Knowing without doing is like plowing without sowing.
AUTHOR UNKNOWN

Some people have a thousand reasons why they
cannot do something, but all you need is
one reason why you can.
DR. DENIS WAITLEY

What is the horizon but the limit of our current vision?
UNKNOWN

Reality can destroy the dream;
why shouldn't the dream destroy reality?
GEORGE MOORE

The road to success is always under construction.
AUTHOR UNKNOWN

When we cannot act as we wish, we must act as we can.
TERRENCE

Faith = Going as far as you can with the light you have.
UNKNOWN

Hear one man before you answer. Hear several men
before you decide.There is no such thing as a self-made person.
I have had much help and have found that if you are
willing to work, many people are willing to help you.
O. WAYNE ROLLINS

Believe and receive. Doubt and do without.
DR. ROBERT SCHULLER

Small minded people talk about people.
Average minded people talk about events.
Great minded people talk about things to come.
ANONYMOUS

I would rather see a crooked furrow than an
unplowed field. I would rather attempt something
great and fail than to attempt nothing and succeed.
DR. ROBERT SCHULLER

**The reasonable man adapts
himself to the world. The
unreasonable one persists in
trying to adapt the world
to himself. All progress
depends on the unreasonable man.**
GEORGE BERNARD SHAW

There's always room at the top.
CHARLES YOUNTS, BUSINESSMAN

Life is but a day at most.
BURNS

Impossible is a word found only in the dictionary of fools.
NAPOLEON

Hell is truth seen too late.
H.G. ADAMS

The greatest truths are the simplest. So are the greatest men.
ANONYMOUS

The true art of memory is the art of attention.
MEMORY EXPERT

Progress always involves risk. You can't steal
second base with one foot on first.
FRED B. WILCOX

No problem can stand the assault of sustained thinking.
VOLTAIRE

It is personalities, not principles, that move the age.
OSCAR WILDE

English laws punish vice. Chinese laws do more.
They reward virtue.
GOLDSMITH

Nature of men is always the same.
It is their habits that separate them.
CONFUCIUS

The purpose of man is an action and not a thought
though it were the noblest.
CALVIN COOLIDGE

I shall be telling this with a sigh ages and ages hence.
Two roads diverged in the wood and I took the
one less traveled and that has made all the difference.
ROBERT FROST

If you can dream it, then you can achieve it.
You will get all you want in life if you help
enough other people get what they want.
ZIG ZIGLAR

To know and not to do is not yet to know.
ZEN SAYING

Wherever anything is being accomplished it is
being done by a mono-maniac with a mission.
PETER DRUCKER

When you create desire, you also create
the ability to complete that desire to go.
DR. ROBERT SCHULLER

There is no security in this earth. There is only opportunity.
DOUGLAS MACARTHUR

Everyone is my superior in that I may learn from them.
ANONYMOUS

Yesterday is past history. Tomorrow may never come.
Today is all we have. Yesterday is a cancelled check.
Tomorrow is a promissory note. Today is all the cash we have.
Spend it like crazy.
ANONYMOUS

Don't let opinions of the average man sway you. Dream and
he thinks you are crazy. Succeed and he thinks you are greedy.
Pay no attention. He simply doesn't understand.
ROBERT G. ALLEN

Nothing is put into this world in full bloom. First there is a seed,
then there is a sprout, then there is a blade, and then a flower.
First there's a baby, then there's a child, and then an adult.
Process is God's law for nature and for man.
JOHN R. CLAYPOOL

The world breaks all people. In the end, some
people are stronger in broken places.
UNKNOWN

You reap what you sow.
APOSTLE PAUL

Some people look at the world as it is and ask why.
I dream of worlds that never were and ask why not.
GEORGE BERNARD SHAW

Integrity has no need of laws.
ALBERT CAMUS

Ultimately we know deeply that other side of fear is freedom.
MARILYN FERGUSON

No person is so free who has not mastered himself.
EPECTELUS

It's not the number of hours put in a day.
It's what you put into those hours.
ANONYMOUS

We know too much and are convinced of too little.
T. S. ELIOT

Best people are often molded out of faults.
SHAKESPEARE

Intent and not the deed is in our power, and therefore,
he who dares greatly does greatly.
ROBERT BROWNING

Anger is only one letter short of danger.
SOMEONE WITH NOT ENOUGH TO DO

A path with no obstacles leads nowhere.
UNKNOWN

Success seems to be largely a matter of hanging on
after all others have let go.
WILLIAM FEATHER

We become what we think about.
THE OLDEST PHILOSOPHY KNOWN

Life is a ladder. Each step is either up or down. It would
be a shame to climb the ladder of success just to
find out it was leaning against the wrong house.
STEPHEN COVEY

A wise man will make more opportunities than he finds.
SIR FRANCIS BACON, 1625

**Keep away from people
who try to belittle your
ambition. Small people
always do that, but the
really great make you feel
that you, too, can become great.**
MARK TWAIN

One man with courage makes a majority.
ANDREW JACKSON

Excellence is never granted to a person but
as the reward of labor.
SIR JOSHUA REYNOLDS

He conquers who endures.
PERSIUS

Luckily, most of my problems have never occurred.
MARK TWAIN

Dumb questions are easier than dumb mistakes.
A TEACHER

Human beings can alter their lives by
altering the attitudes of their mind.
WILLIAM JAMES

God gives us faces and we create our expressions.
AUTHOR UNKNOWN

A performance is worth a world of promise.
AUTHOR UNKNOWN

Gentlemen, never never never never never never never never
(repeat 51 times) quit.
WINSTON CHURCHILL

I can do all things through Christ who strengthens me.
APOSTLE PAUL

Learn from other peoples' mistakes because you'll never have
time to make them all yourself.
UNKNOWN

You'll never fail until you quit trying.
UNKNOWN

Behind brilliant ideas you usually find brilliant people.
CONWAY STONE

Behind every successful man, you will find a surprised mother-in-law.
A SON-IN-LAW

Nothing ever happens until someone sells something.
ZIG ZIGLAR

The quickest way to acquire self-confidence is to do
what you're afraid of.
TOM SCHUFF

Our aspirations are our possibilities.
ROBERT BROWNING

The secret to a successful life is for man to be ready
for his opportunity when it comes.
BENJAMIN DISRAELI

All virtue lies in individual action, in inward reward, in self
determination. There's no moral worth in being swept
away by the crowd even toward the best objective.
UNKNOWN

Celebrate the colors of life and ignore the details.
The details are always vulgar.
OSCAR WILDE

Do unto others as you would have them do unto you.
THE GOLDEN RULE

Life is hard by the yard, but it's a cinch by the inch.
DR. ROBERT SCHULLER

Someday I hope to enjoy enough of what the world calls success
so that someone will ask me, "What is the secret of success?"
And I will simply answer, "I get up when I fall down."
PAUL HARVEY

He who throws mud loses ground.
UNKNOWN

One great strong unselfish soul in every community
could actually redeem the world.
ELBERT HUBBARD

The road to hell is paved with good intentions.
KARL MARX

If the going is easy, you may be going down hill.
UNKNOWN

Children need more models than critics.
A PARENT
Ideas won't work unless you do.
UNKNOWN

Nobody raises his own reputation by lowering other
people's reputations.
UNKNOWN

If you don't know where you are going,
any road will take you there.
UNKNOWN

Smooth sailing never made a skillful sailor.
EARL NIGHTINGALE

A smile only takes 13 muscles. A frown takes 64.
KINGS ISLAND AMUSEMENT PARK

People don't fail. They simply give up.
UNKNOWN

2/3 of promotion is motion.
UNKNOWN

The only way some people exercise their minds is
by jumping to conclusions.
CULLEN HIGHTOWER

Courage is not simply one of the virtues, but the
form of every virtue at the testing point.
C.S. LEWIS

Without courage, wisdom bears no fruit.
BALTASAR GRACIAN

I have learned that successful living is like playing the violin.
It must be practiced daily.
65 YEAR OLD BUSINESSMAN

It's not the critic who counts, not the man who
points out how the strong man has stumbled or
where the doer of deeds could have done them
better. The credit belongs to the man
who is actually in the arena, whose face
is marred by dust, sweat, and blood, who
strives valiantly, who errs and comes
short again and again, who knows the
great enthusiasms and the great
devotions, who spends himself in a
worthy cause, who at best knows in the
end the triumph of high achievement,
and who at the worst if he fails, at least fails
while daring greatly so that his place shall
never be among those timid souls
who know neither victory nor defeat.
THEODORE ROOSEVELT

Self discipline is actually a form of self indulgence.
Self discipline allows you to focus on the
things you want to accomplish.
DR. STAN FRAGER

In spite of everything, I still believe people are really good at heart.
ANNE FRANK

Every great achievement was once considered impossible.
AUTHOR UNKNOWN

Although men have a common destiny, each individual
also has to work out his own personal salvation for himself
in fear and trembling. (Bible) We can help one another
to find the meaning of life, no doubt, but in the last analysis, the
individual is responsible for living his own life and for
"finding himself." If he persists in shifting his responsibilities to
someone else, he fails to find out the meaning of his
own existence. You cannot tell me who I am. I cannot
tell you who you are. If you do not know your own identity,
who is going to identify you?
THOMAS MERTON

No man is an island of itself.
Each is a piece of the continent, a part of the main.
JOHN DONNE

Whenever I decided something with kindness,
I usually made the right decision.
80 YEAR OLD LADY

Courage is like love. It must have hope for nourishment.
NAPOLEON

I have learned that everyone has something to teach.
51 YEAR OLD MAN

The paradox of courage is that a man must be a little careless
of his life even in order to keep it.
G.K. CHESTERTON

Laud not what you are, but what you may become.
CERVANTES

He who isn't busy being born is busy dying.
BOB DYLAN

Aimlessness is a vice.
UNKNOWN

I have learned that optimists live longer than pessimists.
That's why I'm an optimist.
84 YEAR-OLD LADY

We grow only when we push ourselves beyond
what we already know.
ANONYMOUS

Mind is the master. Power that molds and makes man is mind and
evermore he takes, the tool of thought and shaping what he wills,
brings forth a thousand joys, a thousand ills. He thinks in secret
and it comes to pass. Environment is but his looking glass.
JAMES ALLEN

Most people are anxious to improve their circumstances, but are
unwilling to improve themselves. They, therefore, remain bound
to their circumstances.
JAMES ALLEN

Any man's death diminishes me because
I am involved in mankind.
JOHN DONNE

Many people talk like philosophers and live like fools.
H.G. BOHN

No one is so wrong as the man who knows all the answers.
THOMAS MERTON

What everybody sees as true today may turn
out to be false tomorrow.
HENRY DAVID THOREAU

A half-truth is a whole lie.
GHANDI

It is easier to fight for principles than to live by them.
ALFRED ADLER

A fool is his own informer.
YIDDISH PROVERB

If I can stop one heart from breaking, I shall not have
lived in vain. If I can ease one life from aching, or cool one life
from pain, or help one fainting robin into the nest again,
I shall not have lived in vain.
EMILY DICKINSON

The finger of God never leaves identical fingerprints.
STANISLAUS LEC

I have yet to find a person who did not work better and
put forth better effort under a spirit of approval rather
than a spirit of criticism.
CHARLES SCHWAB

No great man lives in vain. The history of the
world is but a biography of great men.
THOMAS CARLYLE

Poverty is the mother of crime.
ROMAN HISTORIAN, 525 B.C.

Men of reason have endured; men of passion have lived.
SEBASTIAN ROCH NICHOLAS CHAMFORT, 1784

To think is to differ.
CLARENCE DARROW, JULY 1925

No one can possibly achieve real success by being a conformist.
J. PAUL GETTY

**You can't build a
reputation on what
you are going to do.**
HENRY FORD

There is no elevator to success. You have to take the stairs.
UNKNOWN

A mind stretched by a new idea,
cannot go back to its original dimensions.
OLIVER WENDELL HOLMES

No generalization is wholly true. Not even this one.
OLIVER WENDELL HOLMES

The great pleasure in life is doing what
people say you cannot do.
WALTER BAGEHOT

Carpe Diem. Seize the day and put as little trust as
you can into tomorrow.
HORNACE ROMAN POET, 15 B.C.

He who lives in fear will never be a free man.
HORNACE ROMAN POET, 15 B.C.

Learn what is true in order that you may do what is right.
THOMAS H. HUXLEY

There is no worse lie than a truth misunderstood
by those who hear it.
WILLIAM JAMES

The difference between a good man and a bad one is choice.
WILLIAM JAMES

Many people think they are thinking when in reality
they are rearranging their prejudices.
WILLIAM JAMES

The worst bankruptcy in the world is the
man who has lost his enthusiasm.
H. W. ARNOLD

No one ever became great by imitation.
SAMUEL JOHNSON

The person with God on his/her own side is a majority.
JOHN KNOX

You can do anything if you have enthusiasm. Enthusiasm is the
yeast that makes your hopes rise to the stars. Enthusiasm is the
spark in your eye, the swing in your gait, the grip of your hand, the
irresistible surge of your will and your energy to execute your ideas.
Enthusiasts are fighters, they have fortitude, they have staying
qualities. Enthusiasm is at the bottom of all progress! With it,
there is accomplishment. Without it, there are only alibis.
HENRY FORD

If you want something done, ask a busy person.
BENJAMIN FRANKLIN

Great works are performed not by strength, but by perseverance.
SAMUEL JOHNSON

It is sobering to consider that when Mozart was my age
he had already been dead for a year.
TOM LEHRER

The man who says "it can't be done" is often interrupted
by a man who is doing it.
CHINESE PROVERB

An idea that is not dangerous is unworthy to be called an idea at all.
ELBERT HUBBARD, 1901

Only passions, great passions, can elevate the soul to great things.
DENIS DIDEROT

What the human mind can conceive and believe, it can accomplish.
WILLIAM JAMES

The height of your accomplishment will equal
the depth of your convictions.
WALTER BAGEHOT

People who are unable to motivate themselves must
be content with mediocrity, no matter how
impressive their other talents.
ANDREW CARNEGIE

Nothing great was ever achieved without enthusiasm.
RALPH WALDO EMERSON

There is no fun in medicine, but there is a lot of medicine in fun.
ANONYMOUS

An obstacle is something you see when you take your
eyes off of your goal.
ANONYMOUS

Forget goals. Value the process.
JAMES BOUTON

Without some goal and some effort to reach it, no man can live.
FEODOR DOSTOEVSKI

I find the greatest thing in this world is not so much where we
stand, as in what directions we are moving.
OLIVER WENDELL HOLMES

Goals are dreams with deadlines.
DIANA S. HUNT

The world stands aside to let anyone pass who knows where he is going.
DAVID S. JORDAN

The tragedy of life doesn't lie in not reaching your goal.
The tragedy lies in having no goal to reach.
BENJAMIN E. MAYS

To be great is to be misunderstood.
RALPH WALDO EMERSON

When you fly like an eagle, you attract the hunters.
MILTON GOULD

The secret of success is constancy of purpose.
BENJAMIN DISRAELI

The first rule of winning. Don't beat yourself.
FOOTBALL ADAGE

Most dreams of glory are safe, because we never
venture to put them into practice.
CHARLES CUROTHE

Quality is never an accident; it is always the
result of intelligent efforts.
JOHN RUSKIN

Genius is one per cent inspiration and 99 percent perspiration.
THOMAS EDISON

What value do you have if you gain the whole
world and loose your own soul?
JESUS CHRIST

**In the arena of human life,
the honors and reward
fall to those who show
their good qualities in action.**
ARISTOTLE

"Mrs. Keller is there anything worse than being blind?"
She replied, "Yes, to be able to see and not have a vision."
TONY ROBBINS

Four out of five doctors don't trust that fifth doctor!
GARY APPLE

"It's difficult to sail, when wind is small."
PHILOSOPHY FROM THE SEA—JAPAN

God and soldier we adore in time of trouble and not before.
MILITARY SAYING

"When God calls you to do a task, take it.
For God will always carry the heavy end."
AN OLD SCOTTISH SAYING

Not making a decision is in fact a decision.
ANONYMOUS

Heaven never helps the man who will not act.
SOPHOCLES

People demand freedom of speech to make up for the
freedom of thought which they avoid.
KIERKEGAARD

Judge a man by his questions rather than his answers.
VOLTAIRE

Giving people a little more than they expect is a good way
to get back a lot more than you'd expect.
ROBERT HALF

The size of the attendance at your funeral will
be determined by the weather.
A WISE MORTICIAN

You probably wouldn't worry about what people think of you
if you could know how seldom they do.
OLIN MILLER

It is a wonderful feeling when you discover some
evidence to support your beliefs.
ANONYMOUS

The highest reward for a person's toil is not
what he gets for it, but what he becomes by it.
JOHN RUSKIN

We have to live today by what truth we can get today
and be ready tomorrow to call it falsehood.

WILLIAM JAMES

If I have been able to see farther than others, it was because
I stood on the shoulders of giants.

ISAAC NEWTON

A firm belief attracts facts. They come out of holes in
the ground and cracks in the walls to support
belief, but the facts run from doubt.

FINLEY POTTER DUNNE

Thinking is the hardest work there is. Which is the probable
reason why so few people engage in it.

HENRY FORD

If anyone can do anything in the world, you can too.

TONY ROBBINS

There is more to this life than can be found in your philosophy.

HAROTICO

Trust your own judgement, for it is your most reliable counselor.
A man's mind has sometimes a way of telling him
more than seven watchmen posted on a high tower.

ECCLESIASTICUS

Never underestimate the power of a small group
of people to change the world. Indeed that is the
way the world has always been changed.

MARGARET MEAD

The hardest thing in the world to understand is the income tax.

ALBERT EINSTEIN

What recommends commerce to me is its enterprise and bravery.
It does not clasp its hands and pray to Jupiter.
HENRY DAVID THOREAU

Experience is the comb that nature gives us after we are bald.
BELGIAN PROVERB

"When wind is small, captain must be good"
PHILOSOPHY FROM THE SEA—JAPAN

Hope is desire and expectation rolled into one.
AMBROSE BIERCE

When one door closes another door opens; but we
often look so long and so regretfully upon the closed
door that we do not see the ones which have opened for us.
ALEXANDER GRAHAM BELL

Make it a point to do something every day that you don't
want to do. This is the golden rule for acquiring the
habit of doing your duty without pain.
MARK TWAIN

Every luxury must be paid for, and everything is a luxury,
starting with being in the world.
CAESAR PAVESE

No one can help another person without helping himself.
RALPH WALDO EMERSON

Getting even with somebody is no way to
get ahead of anybody.
CULLEN HIGHTOWER

If you think education is expensive, try ignorance.
UNKNOWN

A thought that does not result in action is nothing much, and an action that does not proceed from a thought is nothing at all.
GEORGES BERNANOS

It is easy to be brave from a safe distance.
AESOP

Only a person who has faith in himself can be faithful to others.
ERICH FROMM

It is not safe to sit in judgment upon another person's illusion when you are not on the inside. While you are thinking it is just a dream, he may be knowing it is a planet.
MARK TWAIN

Whatever you can do, or dream you can begin it. Boldness has genius, power and magic in it. Begin now!
GOETHE

Every politician, when he leaves office, ought to go straight to jail and serve his time.
FOLK SAYING

The power of an idea can be measured by the degree of resistance it attracts.
DAVID YOHO

When Vince Lombardi said "Sit Down!" I didn't even look for a chair.
BART STARR

Whatever liberates our spirit without giving us
self-control is disastrous.

GOETHE

It is better to wear out than to rust out.

RICHARD CUMBERLAND

Leadership is action; not position.

DONALD H. MCGANNON

There are two things to aim at in life: first, to get
what you want; and after that, to enjoy it.
Only the wisest of mankind achieve the second.

LOGAN PEARSHALL SMITH

No one ever drowns by falling in the water,
they only drown if they stay there.

JOE SABAH

In dreams begins responsibility.

WILLIAM B. YEATS

The greatest piece of real estate you own is the
6" between your ears.

UNKNOWN

Dogs come when they're called;
cats take a message and get back to you.

MARY BLY

The companies of the future will be places of personal fulfillment
for talented people who can contribute to the good of the
organization. These companies will also be led by strong leaders
with vision and a commitment to practical action.

CONWAY STONE

The Indian scout was sent ahead to view the horizon.
We need more horizon leaders looking for the
best way into the future.
CONWAY STONE

It's choice not chance that determines destiny.
CONWAY STONE

They may kill the dreamers, like they did Kennedy, King, Ghandi
and Lincoln. But I am convinced that as long as you and I follow
our God given dreams, they will never kill the dream.
CONWAY STONE

Choice and death are two sides of the same coin.
Each choice we choose involves the death of
thousands of other opportunities. Therefore, choose
carefully, and let the other options die.
CONWAY STONE

Plant trees under which you will never sit.
CONWAY STONE

Success is achieved by choosing well.
CONWAY STONE

Contemplation without action is to be unjust to yourself.
CONWAY STONE

A mistake proves that someone stopped talking
long enough to do something.
CONWAY STONE

The meaning of life is to love God.
CONWAY STONE

We are not a product of our environment;
we are a product of our response to our environment.
UNKNOWN

If you can dream it, you can do it.
Always remember that this whole
thing was started with a mouse.
WALT DISNEY

Where there is no gardener, there is no garden.
UNKNOWN

The enemy of the "best" is the "good."
UNKNOWN

In great attempts, it is glorious even to fall.
CASSIUS

High aims bring out high character
and great dreams bring out great minds.
TYRONE EDWARDS

Every man believes he has a greater possibility.
RALPH WALDO EMERSON

If you lower your standards, you deserve everything you get.
THOMAS MELOHN

Ambition is the shadow of a dream.
WILLIAM SHAKESPEARE

Try not to become a man of success,
but rather try to become a man of value.
ALBERT EINSTEIN

We must overcome the notion that we must
be regular. It robs us of the chance to be
extraordinary and leads us to the mediocre.

UTA HAGEN

The only real risk is the risk of thinking too small.

FRANCIS M. LAPPE

And the trouble is, if you don't
risk anything, you risk even more.

ERICA M. JONG

The real risk is in doing nothing.

DENIS WAITLEY

The means by which we
live have outdistanced the
ends for which we live.
Our scientific power has
outrun our spiritual power.
We have fueled missiles
and misguided men.

DR. MARTIN LUTHER KING, JR.

Our achievements of today are but the sum
total of our thoughts of yesterday. You are
today where your thoughts of yesterday
have brought you, and you will be tomorrow
where your thoughts of today take you.

BLAISE PASCAL

Dare to be wrong and to dream.

FREIDRICH SCHILLER

My grandfather always said that living
is like licking honey off a thorn.
LOUIS ADAMIC

Wise men learn more from fools
than fools learn from wise men.
MARCUS PORCIOUS CATO

We must either find a way or make one.
HANNIBAL

Great men are meteors designed to burn
so that the earth may be lightened.
NAPOLEON BONAPARTE

To be trusted is a greater complement than to be loved.
GEORGE MACDONALD

A zealous sense of mission is only possible
when there is opposition to it.
D.W. EWING

I hold it that a little rebellion now and then is a good thing.
THOMAS JEFFERSON

If you're not failing every now and again,
it's a sign you're not doing anything very innovative.
WOODY ALLEN

Ships are safe in harbor, but that's not what ships are for.
COUNTRY MUSIC SAYING

As you enter positions of trust and power,
dream a little before you think.
TONI MORRISON

Strategic planning is worthless — unless
there is first a strategic vision.
JOHN NAISBITT

A rock pile ceases to a rock pile the moment
a single man contemplates it, bearing within
him the image of a cathedral
ANTONIE DE SAINT-EXUPERY

Commitment unlocks the doors of imagination;
it allows us and gives us the "right stuff"
to turn our dreams into reality.
JAMES WOMACK

Vision looks inward and becomes a duty.
Vision looks outward and becomes aspiration.
Vision looks upward and becomes faith.
STEPHEN WISE

A person is not old until regret takes the place of dreams.
JOHN BARRYMORE

Without some goal and some effort to reach it, no man can live.
FEODOR DOSTOEVSKI

You're on the road to success when you
realize that failure is merely a detour.
ANONYMOUS

The ability to convert ideas to things is the
secret of outward success.
HENRY WARD BEACHER

He who mounts a wild elephant
goes where the elephant goes.
RANDOLPH BOURNE

If you break one hundred, watch your golf.
If you break eighty, watch your business.
JOEY ADAMS

In the final analysis, everyone is in business for himself.
ANONYMOUS

Consultant is a man who knows fifty ways to make love
but doesn't know any women.
ANONYMOUS

You cannot plow a field by turning it over in your mind.
ANONYMOUS

Think like a man of action and act like a man of thought.
HENRI BERGSON

In order to act, you must be somewhat insane.
A reasonable, sensible man is satisfied with thinking.
GEORGE CLEMENCEAU

An ounce of action is worth a ton of theory.
RICK ENGLES

In the simplest terms, a leader is one who knows
where he wants to go, and gets up and goes.
JOHN ERSKINE

Genius is ability to put into effect what is in your mind.
SCOTT FITZGERALD

If you can give your son or daughter
one gift, let it be enthusiasm.
BRUCE BARTON

Enthusiasm is the greatest asset in the world.
It beats money, power, and influence.
HENRY CHESTER

Enthusiasm reflects confidence, spreads
good cheer, raises morale, inspires associates,
arouses loyalty, and laughs at adversity…it is beyond price.
ALLEN COX

Enthusiasm is at the bottom of all progress! With it there is
accomplishment. Without it, there are only alibis.
HENRY FORD

The voice of the intellect is
a soft one, but it does not
rest until it has gained
a hearing. Ultimately, after
endless rebuffs, it succeeds.
This is one of the few
points at which one may
be optimistic about
the future of mankind.
SIGMUND FREUD

The secret of genius is to carry the
spirit of the child into old age,
which means never losing your enthusiasm.
ALDOUS HUXLEY

A hero is no braver than an ordinary man,
but he is braver five minutes longer.
RALPH WALDO EMERSON

A leader is a dealer in hope.
NAPOLEON BONAPARTE

The people who have changed the universe
have never accomplished it by changing officials,
but always by inspiring the people.
NAPOLEON BONAPARTE

The prime function of a leader is to keep hope alive.
JOHN W. GARDNER

Leadership is action not position.
DONALD MCGANNON

If you play it safe in life, you've decided
you don't want to grow anymore.
SHIRLEY HUFSTEDLER

"That which we persist in doing becomes easier to do."
RALPH WALDO EMERSON

No man becomes suddenly different from his
habit and cherished thought.
COMMANDER JOSHUA L. CHAMBERLAIN

Dreams are the touchstones of Character.
HENRY DAVID THOREAU

If a man is called to be a street sweeper, he should sweep streets
even as Magellan painted or as Shakespeare wrote poetry or as
Beethoven composed music. He should sweep streets so well that
all the host of heaven and earth will pause to say, "Here lived a
great street sweeper who did his job well."
DR. MARTIN LUTHER KING, JR.